ANGEL FACE

First published in 1999 by
Marino Books
an imprint of Mercier Press
16 Hume Street Dublin 2
Tel: (01) 6615299; Fax: (01) 6618583
E.mail: books@marino.ie
Trade enquiries to CMD Distribution
55A Spruce Avenue
Stillorgan Industrial Park
Blackrock County Dublin
Tel: (01) 294 2556; Fax: (01) 294 2564
E.mail: cmd@columba.ie

© Sheila Connolly Danziger 1999

ISBN 1 86023 087 3

10 9 8 7 6 5 4 3 2 1
A CIP record for this title is available
from the British Library

Cover design by SPACE
Printed in Ireland by ColourBooks,
Baldoyle Industrial Estate, Dublin 13

ANGEL FACE

A MEMOIR

SHEILA CONNOLLY DANZIGER

ACKNOWLEDGEMENTS

To my husband Harry Lee for his unconditional love and for believing in me

To our late brother Timmy. I am sure he is making beautiful music in heaven with John McCormack and a chorus of angels.

To my sisters Maureen, Paddy, Dolores and Joan. Now we can stop talking about it and read about it.

To my daughters Bridget, Erin and Dolly for their support and love

Thanks also to Danny Danziger, to Patrick McCabe for getting the ball rolling, to Sidney Sheldon for his encouragement in the past years and to Rosemary Dawson

Dedicated to our mother Violet and her young son Victor, whose spirits hoped for that peace which a cruel and merciless world never afforded them

We have been beautiful
We have been young

CONTENTS

PROLOGUE

EVICTION

Ireland 1936. Times were tough. We were in a bad way because my father had no job. Nor had he any hopes of one. The rent had not been paid for some time. Late afternoon on 16 November, the police banged on the door of our little terraced house in Brownstown, County Kildare. Timmy and I went to the door. I remember it was raining because I could hear the rain darting off their capes. I remember the glint of the peak of their caps in the pale winter light. One of the policemen had a big handlebar moustache which I could not take my eyes off. Timmy was fascinated by it. The big policeman glared coldly at us.

'Is your father home, child?' he bellowed at me. I shook my head, unable to answer. Daddy was never home. 'Mama, Mama.' She detected the fear in my voice and rushed to my side. 'Shush, Sheila, it'll be all right.' I clung to her skirt. But I still remember the look of terror in her face when he unrolled the eviction notice that required us to leave with immediate effect. She pleaded with them. Then, in vain, she frantically tried to shut the door on them. But they forced their way in and invaded our little home.

Mama was trying desperately to grab some clothes and pots and pans while they roared at her to get out and take her brood with her. She ignored them. Victor was wailing and Paddy and Maureen were screaming, 'You leave our Mama alone!' Timmy and I ran into the pantry and I told Timmy to put his fingers in his ears. He was shaking. Paddy came looking for us in a panic and told us to hurry or we'd be left behind. The police were shouting at us to get out *now*. Maureen, Joan and Dolores were helping Mama fetch blankets. Then Mama handed us clothes and told us to put them on over what we were wearing. I put on two dresses, a smock, a sweater and my Sunday coat. We were like little Michelin men. My mother bundled Victor into the old black Victorian pram and lifted Timmy in alongside him.

We were flung out the door. So off we went at a great pace out into the lashing rain and down the wet grey road. I looked back to see the police boarding up the windows and doors of our house. They were hammering nails into the wooden planks that crossed the windows. The neighbours just stared out from behind the net curtains on their windows. I told Mama and she just said, 'Sheila, don't mind them.' Not one of them came to help us. They were afraid to because many of them were in similar circumstances. Tomorrow it could be one of them.

We were all carrying our belongings. Joan and Dolores were assigned some smaller pots and pans, while Mama tied the big ones onto the pram. Paddy and Maureen carried the blankets – they were trying to keep them dry by putting them inside their open coats. Mama then tied string around their waists to keep the blankets in position.

We looked worse than a bunch of tinkers, though Paddy said at least the tinkers had a lovely warm, dry caravan. We had no idea where we were going. I was worried Daddy wouldn't be able to find us. 'Well, he'll just have to look, won't he?' Mama had muttered. I had never seen her so distraught. Her hair had fallen out of its normally tidy bob. We were stumbling along the road aimlessly. The big spokes of the pram were squeaking in the rain and squelching through the mud. The wind was rising now and darkness was falling. My hair was sticking to my face. 'Mama, I can't see,' I said. Maureen brushed my hair back out of my eyes, grabbed my hand and told me to hold tight, to shush and not be annoying Mama.

Then there was a loud clap of thunder and a flash of white lightning darted across the sky. I was terrified. 'Run, children, run,' Mama said. But I couldn't. I felt too heavy under the weight of my wet clothes to move. My legs were tired and numb. Mama lifted me into the pram with Victor and Timmy. For a minute it almost toppled over. Timmy was clinging so tight I couldn't breathe. But I didn't care because I felt safe in there. At least this way I wouldn't get left behind. We bobbed up and down along the bumpy road with the saucepans clanging off the pram. At one point, we took shelter under a great big old tree. But the lightning was so close that my mother decided to keep going; trees were dangerous in storms.

Then suddenly Maureen and Dolores said to Mama, 'Why don't we try the old schoolhouse?' Before you could count to ten we had turned down a little laneway off the main road. In the distance we could see the outline of the derelict house. Mama sent Maureen and Paddy ahead to look inside. A few minutes later, Maureen shouted at us to come on, calling out, 'Mama, there's nobody here.'

'Thank the Lord,' whispered my mother. We pushed back the creaking rotten door and stumbled inside. What a relief to get in from the dark, stormy night. We entered a large room that Mama declared must have been the classroom. It had a fireplace and two small windows with broken panes that looked out onto the road beyond. There were old stairs leading to a second floor. Mama told us to follow her upstairs. It was very cold in there. We sat huddled together on the floor. There were some little kittens running about with a mother cat. We felt scared and lost.

Mama made us take off our wet clothes and wrapped us in the blankets, which were a bit drier. Miraculously, there were a few small sods of turf near the fire which must have been left by the last occupants. Maureen and Paddy went off to find my father to tell him where we were. Soon the fire built up and Timmy and I huddled up in front of the heat while Mama fed Victor. After a while we all fell asleep, exhausted by our ordeal.

We were woken by Maureen and Paddy, who had accompanied my father home. They had found him in the pub and were determined to drag him back. He brought some food. God knows where he had got it from. We didn't care. Very soon there was a delicious smell of bacon frying in the pan. Timmy was chewing on his old jacket in anticipation of the food. We ate off the saucepan lids. We had left our plates behind in our hasty exit.

I remember Joan and Paddy fighting over who would get a lid first. Suddenly one of the kittens ran over to the fireplace and tried to pull a piece of bacon out of the pan. My father yelled and grabbed the screaming kitten by the neck. 'Daddy, no! Please don't, Daddy! Daddy ... !' we cried. Maureen ran to stop him. I can still hear the kitten's tortured cry. My father strangled it in front of us. Then he callously hurled its little limp body across the room. We were terrified. He threw the cat and the rest of the kittens out the door of the house. Timmy and I clung to each other, shaking. I started retching; I couldn't swallow. My mother just sat there silently weeping as she rocked Victor back and forth in her lap.

During the night the wind howled through the big empty schoolroom. It whistled under the gap in the front door and kept blowing the door open. Daddy got up and tried to bang it shut but the latch was broken. I kept waking up and hearing scratching noises. Now that the cats had gone, the rats came in and scurried across the room throughout the night. We children were petrified. And every now and then as the thunder clapped, the lightning would brighten up the room in a deathly pale light. The storm seemed to rage on and off all night. To this day, I have nightmares about that night.

The next morning the room was very quiet and still. The storm had ceased. As we lay in our blankets, I saw my mother move across to Victor's pram. All at once, her shrill scream filled the room. She was crying, 'The baby's dead; Victor's dead!' She kept repeating this over and over as she rocked his cold little body in her arms.

After a while, my father left the house, returning later

with two men and a cart. It held a small white coffin. Maureen and I were looking out of the window and there were some children standing outside. 'Go away,' my sister sobbed.

Victor was gently laid in the coffin and the lid was nailed shut. I kept thinking he would wake up and be frightened. Then my mother and father climbed up into the rickety cart pulled by an old grey mare. They held the little white coffin between them. As we watched from the window, I heard one of the men say, 'There are rat bites all over him.' Then they lightly tapped the horse and disappeared down the road with the coffin wobbling on the back of the cart. Ever since then I have been terrified of rats and I sometimes dream they are biting my hands while I am sleeping.

I was devastated because I used to walk Victor in his pram. I could not comprehend that he was dead. Victor was only one-and-a-half years of age. He was the third child to die since we had come back to Ireland.

How did we have the misfortune to end up like this? Poor Mama; it was a far cry from her wealthy upbringing.

1

THE STABLE BOY
AND THE GRAND MASTER'S DAUGHTER

My mother, Violet Caroline Thornton, was born in Dublin on 3 November 1903 to William and Susanna Thornton, of well-to-do Protestant stock. She was their first-born. The following year she was joined by a brother, William, who became known as Billy and whom she idolised. Her father, my grandfather William Thornton, lived in a beautiful big Georgian home on the Curragh Camp, County Kildare, the chief Irish military base, which was about a mile or so from the village of Brownstown. He was a well-respected businessman and pillar of the community who owned several stores and was also a coal merchant. He gave employment to a large number of people in the area. More importantly he was a Grand Master of the Freemasons. Her mother, my grandmother Susanna (neé Kirkpatrick), was a champion golfer.

My mother had everything she could wish for as a child, in stark contrast to her later years. She was privately educated by a governess until she was fourteen years old; then she was sent to the Rutherford School for

Violet Thornton, aged 8

Tmothy Connolly

Girls, a boarding school in Sandymount, Dublin. She was very musical – an accomplished pianist with a beautiful singing voice – and trained at the Royal Irish Academy of Music. By all accounts she was a lovely fun-loving and outgoing girl, ill-prepared for the hardships that lay ahead.

My father, Timothy Conleth Connolly, was born in Naas, County Kildare. He was born to parents of a different class and religious persuasion. His parents, my paternal grandparents, Timothy Conleth Connolly and his wife Maryann, were devout Catholics who said the rosary every night. My grandfather was a carpenter who was sadly an alcoholic. My father had a brother Charles and a sister Elizabeth, who was known as Lillie. They lived in a council terrace house on the Naas Road on the way to the Curragh. My father attended the local Catholic national school. When he left school at twelve, he went to work with racehorses at different stud farms.

While my mother was studying music, my father, in total contrast, was what they called 'a jockey boy', a racing apprentice. In 1923, he was working for a jockey who had horses in Brownstown, about a mile or so from the Curragh, where my mother lived. Apparently my mother was friendly with the O'Reidy family, in whose stables my father was working as a stable hand. Daddy had always wanted to be a racehorse trainer and this job was a first step towards that goal for him. One day my mother was riding out at the O'Reidy's, when my father came into the yard.

My father ran over to help her dismount from her charge. He was smitten by this elegant, attractive horse-woman. Her hair was chestnut brown, thick and curly and worn bobbed. She was captivated not only by his dark sultry looks, for he was an extremely handsome man, but also by his charming sense of humour. He was very sallow-skinned, with black hair, deep-brown penetrating eyes and thick black eyebrows. He was slim and short, with a very intense look about him. He used to smoke strong cigarettes called Woodbines, which were tuppence a pack. He often wore a tweed cap, which darkened his eyes even more.

They could not have been more different. She was well-spoken with an educated accent, whereas he had a rougher country accent. They were worlds apart but that seemed only to heighten the attraction between them. They quickly fell in love and she became a frequent visitor to her friends' stables. A secret passionate romance blossomed. To her dismay, my mother became pregnant and my father proposed marriage to her. She was only nineteen years old.

Her parents were outraged when she told them she was pregnant and in love with Timothy Connolly. As far as I know they were the only people in Ireland who ever knew of her condition and they certainly did not want their precious daughter involved with a mere jockey boy who, even worse, was a Catholic. It was potentially humiliating for her father, as Grand Master of the Freemasons, so they would not permit her to marry my father. They were determined to separate the young lovers and dispatched Violet off to America, away from the public eye and well away from the likes of Timothy Connolly. There she had a maternal uncle, by the name of Thomas Kirkpatrick, who had been living and working for some years in Brooklyn,

New York, where he managed a department store. I assume that all the arrangements for her departure were made very hurriedly and secretly. Keen to preserve their daughter's good name, the parents told relatives and friends that Violet was going to further her musical studies in New York.

To say that Mama's parents did not like my father was an understatement. They felt that he had ruined their daughter's life. At nineteen years of age, Violet Thornton had had a bright future. She had a privileged upbringing, a good education, musical talent and the promise of a fine dowry. They had hoped to make a good match for their attractive, talented daughter and they were still hopeful that all was not lost.

And so my mother made the lonely passage from Cobh to New York. She was very ill for most of the voyage. All that kept her going was a letter from my father promising her that he would seek her out as soon as he had made enough money for the voyage. Her Uncle Thomas met her at the docks and brought her to a respectable boarding house for young ladies in the family way. He lived in a rooming house nearby, as did so many single men in those days. And so she began her new life. She continued with her musical studies until such time as her pregnancy became too visible; all the while she lived for my father's letters.

Her family would have been horrified had they known that the young lovers were still in contact with one another. My father's family acted as go-betweens for their letters. My mother's parents had hoped that by moving her across the ocean they could sever all links between the young couple and that in time their precious daughter would forget this unsuitable young man. The plan was that after she had given birth, Violet would put the baby up for adoption and return home to resume her studies at the Royal Irish Academy. But they had not counted on my father following her to America.

I believe my father and mother were truly in love with each other. There was a passionate intensity about him and once he got an idea in his head it was hard to persuade him otherwise. He was determined to follow my mother but he would have had a long wait to enter the United States because of the quota system. I guess it was easier for my mother, as her Uncle Thomas had probably sponsored her and she had the finances to support herself. My father, on the other hand, had no money and nobody to sponsor him. His only hope was to save up to go to Canada first, then enter the United States by crossing over the Canadian border as an illegal immigrant.

Just before he arrived, in January 1924, Mama gave birth to my eldest sister, Maureen. We don't know if Mama knew at that point whether he was on his way or not because post took so long in those days and once he had left Ireland he would have been afraid to contact her because of his illegal status. Lord knows what she went through. But Mama was a very brave and intrepid woman. She must have been put under considerable pressure as an unmarried mother to give up her child for adoption, as her parents had arranged. As it was, her struggles were only beginning. She moved into another boarding house with another young woman in similar circumstances and gave piano lessons to the landlady's daughters in exchange for her room.

To her enormous relief, Timothy Connolly finally

arrived in New York from Canada and contacted her via a mutual friend sometime in the spring of 1924. And so the young lovers were reunited. My mother converted to the Catholic faith and she and my father were married quietly in April 1924. When she wrote to inform her parents, her father had her publicly denounced from the pulpit. One of their flock had strayed and disgraced them. It is hard to imagine how someone could do that to their own daughter today, but they were Freemasons and that is the way it was back then. Her circumstances changed overnight. Worse was to follow; from that day forward she was ignored by her family. Her parents literally disowned her and never saw or communicated with her again. Both her parents died within ten months of each other in 1930–31. So, apart from my father, she was very much on her own.

I sometimes wonder what she had in common with my father. I can't imagine how my mother could have got on with him. Sometimes, when I look at the wistful expression on her face as a child in photographs, I wonder if something happened in her childhood to make her fall for a man like my father? Perhaps Timothy Connolly was in some ways rather like her own father in that he too was a domineering man. He was undeniably persuasive, and my mother was in a very vulnerable condition. The fact that he followed her all the way to America and stood by her probably impressed her very much. It saddens me now to look at photos of her as a child compared to those taken later. There was a look in her eyes even then as if she were unloved.

I suspect she was a loving person and her parents held their children at a distance, as was often the way then. Daddy's youthful zest and passion may have seemed warmer to her. I am sure he was very charming in his youth and certainly different from what she was used to. He had a great sense of humour and was always telling funny stories. He was also very determined. Many people would have been intimidated by the move to America but not my father, who was very fortunate in that nothing frightened him. He was very confident and outgoing and usually got what he wanted. Everyone loved him. Sadly for my mother, as she got to know him she discovered he was a street angel.

They lived in Brooklyn after they married. I do not know what work my father did when he first arrived – he might have worked with horses or as a labourer – but around the end of 1924, my parents went to Pittsburgh, presumably to get some kind of work. By then my mother was pregnant with my sister Patricia (Paddy), who was born in Pittsburgh in August 1925. When exactly they returned to Brooklyn I do not know but my sister Dolores was born there in 1926. Eventually, to their enormous relief, my father got employment as a chauffeur in New York City with a socialite, Mrs Henry James. He was to remain in her household for the next six years.

My parents settled down with their three children, Maureen, Dolores and Paddy, in the Bay Ridge section of Brooklyn, a nice neighbourhood which was predominantly Irish. They also expanded their family, with the births of Joan, myself (Sheila) and my brother Timmy. We lived in an apartment building on an upper floor and since there was no elevator the mothers used to leave the prams under the stairway in the hallway. We children used to play in the entry hallway.

It was while we were still living in America that Maureen remembers getting her first beating from my father. For some reason or other she was sent to Mass by herself and Daddy gave her a dime to put in the collection. I don't know what made her think she could get away with it, but she kept the dime, went to a shoemaker and had taps put on the soles of her shoes. When my father found out what she had done he got a belt and beat her mercilessly while my mother in vain begged him to stop. When he finally stopped he sent Maureen to the bedroom.

Apparently when I was a baby in the pram it was Maureen's job to stroll around outside and push the pram until I fell asleep. Maureen was a bright girl and noticed that I always seemed to fall asleep after I cried. So whenever she was out of Mama's sight she used to slap my hands to make me cry, and sure enough I would fall asleep. Then Maureen would be off in a flash to go and play with the other kids.

My mother had some cousins of her own parents living in Brooklyn. We used to call them Aunt Margaret and Aunt Catherine. I think they were sisters. Aunt Margaret was married to a man named William McKeon, whom we called Uncle Will and who was the manager of a post office in the Bronx. (After we returned to Ireland, Uncle Will used to send us big bundles of comics.) The three of them lived together. Aunt Catherine might have been a widow. We went there to visit them now and again, and on one of these visits Aunt Margaret was downstairs in the basement when we arrived. Maureen still had a cast on her leg from being knocked down by a taxi after another child had pushed her out onto the road. As she attempted to go down to see Aunt Margaret she tripped and fell down the stairs, breaking her left arm. She now had two plaster casts.

In the summer, we used to go to Far Rockaway. We rented a small house close to the beach. I cannot recall much about the place except for the fact that we seemed to be accident-prone when we were there. One day my mother was cooking a pot of stew as we were running around the house. Just after she lifted the pot off the stove and was carrying it towards the table, Maureen ran in front of her, causing her to spill the pot of boiling stew down Maureen's back. Maureen stayed hunched over for a long time after that scalding. It was too painful to straighten up. On another occasion I fell through a rotten boardwalk and a large sliver of wood wedged into my armpit and came out through my shoulder. I was taken by ferry to hospital to have it removed.

There were two reasons why we had to consider returning home to Ireland: one was the Depression and the other was to settle my mother's estate. We were fortunate that our father was not out of work at all during the Depression. In fact we were a lot better off in America than when we came home to Ireland. However, we had other worries. Because of the Depression, illegal aliens were being rounded up and deported. And since my father had come across the border from Canada without the necessary papers he would have been regarded as one of these illegal aliens. He did not want to be deported because if that happened he would not be able to get back into the US. When he was asked on our departure why he was leaving America he said it was 'for the good of my health'.

After my mother's parents died in 1930-31, the estate had to be settled. According to Maureen some settlement was made but we never knew what it was. I don't know if my grandparents had made their wills; they probably hadn't, because as far as they were concerned my mother was no longer their daughter and they would have made sure that she was not to have anything. As it was, there was still some conflict between my mother and her brother about the property.

Paddy, Dolores, Maureen, Joan, Sheila (2) and Timmy (6 months)
Passport photo taken in June 1932

In July 1932 we set sail from New York on a German liner called the *Deutschland*. I remember that we were all dressed alike, with coordinating skirts and middy tops, and little hats in the shape of beanies made of white pie-shaped wedges. Maureen recalls my father telling her to keep a lookout for the Statue of Liberty when we boarded the ship but she does not remember anything about the voyage. There's a passport picture of all of us taken before we left for Ireland. Timmy was six months; I was only two, Joan was four, Paddy was seven, Dolores was six and Maureen was eight. One of the things about that photograph that strikes me is the apprehension in Mama's face, although our parents had hopes about the new and better life they would have back home. But sadly they were in for a shock.

2

BROWNSTOWN

We arrived at Cobh, County Cork, in the south-west of Ireland on a grey misty morning in the summer of 1932. I vaguely remember the excitement of the ship coming into the bay and sailing up through Cork Harbour. I'm told there was a funny-looking car waiting for us on the docks, which made our mother whoop to our father, 'Tim, look at the old tin Lizzie!' Aunt Lillie and her husband Uncle Pat were there to greet us and bring us on the 160-mile journey to Naas. Apparently, Uncle threw me up in the air. We all squeezed into the funny black car, which he must have hired for the day. My sisters remember Mama pointing out cows to us as we scudded across the green countryside, bumping up and down on the red seat in the back. It was the first time we ever saw a cow. Dolores says Uncle made mooing sounds. He was funny and always teasing us. Daddy was thirsty so we had to stop in a hotel for a drink on the way.

The roads weren't great in those days so it was almost nightfall by the time we arrived at Granny Connolly's house in Naas. Granny was dressed in black. She was short but lean, with dark black hair pulled back from her face and tightly coiled into a chignon. She lived in a single-storey terrace council cottage with her daughter Lillie and son-in-law Pat and their two young sons Joe and Jack. The house had only a kitchen, two bedrooms and an outside toilet. I cannot recall where we all slept. With our arrival, thirteen souls were living in that small house. I don't know how we all squeezed into the house that summer but we lived there with them while my mother was negotiating with her brother over her parents' estate. So I guess our stay in Naas was from summer to early September, when school started.

My mother was pregnant when we moved to Browns-town. I often wonder how that happened in a house with as little privacy as we had in Naas. Aunt Lillie was also pregnant. She was short and plump, with black hair pulled back off her face like Granny's. She was quiet and her husband adored her. I know Aunt Lillie was very fond of my mother and they sustained this friendship over the years. Our Uncle Pat was a thin, wiry man with a constant happy smile on his face. He was a darling and so gentle and lovable. He was always very kind to us. But he was strongly against England having the Six Counties in Northern Ireland. He used to say, 'Och they should shoot the crows that fly over the border.'

Shortly after we moved to Brownstown, my mother gave birth to a baby girl, whom she called Susanna, after my maternal grandmother. Susanna lived for only a day or two but still, as was the custom in Ireland, there was a wake. We had a little parlour-cum-living room where Susanna was laid out on the table, which had been covered with a white lace tablecloth. She was dressed in a long white christening dress, her hands were folded and there were little snowdrop flowers between her fingers. She looked like a porcelain doll. I remember it clearly, even though I was only three years old; these things make a big impact when you are little.

My father told me to take Timmy and Joan and go in and kiss Susanna. We didn't want to because we were frightened. Timmy was crying. I remember kissing her on her cold little forehead. Timmy was behind me and would not look at her. I left the parlour with Timmy hanging on to my dress. As we left the room my father glared at us and gave Timmy a swat on the backside. Susanna is buried in Naas in the Connolly family plot. Dolores still has a lock of Susanna's hair; it was black.

I don't know what my granny thought of us. She ran the house with an iron rod and never showed us much affection. I don't know if she even liked my mother. In photographs she looks pretty dour but maybe she had had a hard life. We heard that Grandad had been an alcoholic. They say it runs in families. Maybe Daddy was like him. Later on in my life, I often wondered whether she blamed my mother for my father's leaving Ireland in the first place.

My father's brother Charlie and his wife, Maisie, lived in Dublin. They had four or five children but we rarely saw them. That summer, Uncle Charlie and his family emigrated to Australia. It was at the time when the Australian government was paying the passage of appropriate emigrants to go to their country. The eldest girl, Mary, who was about eighteen, did not go with the others.

Whenever my parents would go off, Mary used to come and stay with us children. It always struck me as strange that my father didn't get a notion to go to Australia after the disappointment of the homecoming and the cramped surroundings of the house.

At the end of the summer, after a long wait, a house to rent finally became available in Brownstown, a little village on the edge of the Curragh. And I suspect Granny wasn't too sorry to see the back of us. Our new home in Brownstown was one of six terrace houses. The front door opened into a long hall; on the right were two bedrooms – the one to the front of the house was our parents' bedroom; the second, to the back of the house, was the children's bedroom. To the left of the hall was the kitchen and a large pantry.

The great thing about living in the middle of the village was that we made lots of friends with the other kids around. They used to tease us about our accents and we were known as the little Yanks. We traded with each other. They taught us new games on condition that we showed them some American ones. We also traded American expressions and swear words for the odd bull's-eye or gobstopper.

Shortly after we arrived in Brownstown, Maureen learned how to ride a bicycle on the sidewalk in front of the house. It was an adult bike not a kiddie's one, so she could not reach the seat. She looked so small on that big bike but she was determined to learn. At the start, Mama used to help balance the bike, but one day she let go and after a few tries Maureen was off on her own. My sister was so proud when she had learned how to ride a bike. A few years later, Maureen taught me. I'll never forget the sheer exhilaration of it. I used to love the freedom of cycling down country lanes with the wind blowing in my hair and billowing through my dress.

Daddy got a job on the Curragh soon after we went to live in Brownstown and life settled down for a while. He always wanted to train racehorses so he bought a race-horse, which he called Bay Ridge. It ran in several races but never won anything. In the end, he had to sell it. One of the most convenient amenities for our parents was the bookie's office next door. My mother was fond of the odd flutter. I believe that her father may also have gambled but perhaps this was hearsay. Mama was also a mean whist player, which did not go down too well with the ladies of the parish!

At first things at Brownstown weren't too bad. We even had a girl who helped my mother with us children. Her name was Annie Doyle. She and her mother had worked in the Thornton house on the Curragh when my mother was a child. My mother's brother Billy, his wife, Madge, and their daughter Angela were now living in our grand-parents' former home. It was quite a large house and the family businesses were still operating after the death of my grandfather. Because Billy was a general's aide in the army, my Aunt Madge and his daughter Angela saw him only when he happened to come to the camp with the general. He just ignored us; if he passed us in the street, he would cross to the other side.

Then our luck began to change again. About a year later my mother gave birth to a stillborn baby. I think this child is buried in the Thornton family plot in Cut Bush. Perhaps this was because the child was never baptised and could not be buried in the Catholic cemetery. When we were living in the terrace house in Brownstown in 1933-36 we had a cow called Daisy that was kept at the O'Reidys' farm near us. It was the place my parents first met. One dark evening my father went to milk the cow and had Maureen go along with him to hold the oil lamp. There was no electricity in the barn. She needed to go to the toilet but he would not let her go before they left the house. While she was holding up the lamp so he could see, Maureen asked him again. But he ignored her so she had to stay there holding the light. Poor Maureen couldn't wait any longer and while she was standing there she wet herself. She cried with shame and fear. Daddy was furious and when we got home he gave her a beating. She can't have been more than maybe nine years of age. She wet the bed every night for a long time after that incident.

On 21 April 1935, Victor was born. I think his proper name might have been William, according to the official parish records. I have a birth certificate for a William Connolly, child of Violet Thornton Connolly and Timothy Connolly. Why he was called Victor, I'll never know. Victor was not a healthy baby. I think he was crippled and delicate because I cannot ever recall his either sitting up alone or trying to walk, all the time he was alive.

Then Daddy lost his job and our lives changed overnight. He was always off somewhere on his bike looking for work and he used to keep this bike in the bedroom. Jobs were scarce and he had a lot of hungry mouths to feed at home. My mother's estate appeared to be nowhere near being resolved. They were bleak times. We started to fall behind with the rent and eventually, on that cold wet November's day, we were evicted and had to squat in the old schoolhouse.

When my grandparents' estate was finally settled between my mother and her brother, Mama used the small inheritance to help my father acquire a large piece of land in Brownstown, on which he started building us a new house. We all helped build that house. When he had the scaffolding up and was pouring the cement in he would throw in anything he could find, such as old bicycle frames and old pots to fill up the cement. Our cat disappeared mysteriously during this time and I often wonder if it fell in there too. My father said that those walls would stand forever.

While the house was being built my mother had returned to Cut Bush and had left behind the building plans. It was a terrible, stormy night. Trees were being uprooted and the rain was pelting down. When my father found out that Mama had not brought the papers back with her he became very angry and hit her. They were constantly arguing. Maureen jumped on his back and said, 'Don't you hit Mama.' He threw her off his back and slapped her. He then turned to Mama and told her to walk back to Brownstown that very minute and get the papers.

In May 1937 we moved from being squatters to homeowners. The new house in Brownstown was finished and we moved back there. We were all very proud of our new home. We called it the Paddock. Daddy also found work again, so life improved for a while. The house had two bedrooms and a kitchen that we virtually lived in. We had no toilet – we roughed it in the bushes. None of the houses on our road had electricity or running water. That came a few years later. The house still stands today and is well maintained. It has since been extended and has a garage and outhouses.

One thing I remember clearly about the new house was that a man used to come to it late at night. I think he was on the run and it seemed to me that he used to come by regularly. There used to be an oil lamp in the kitchen for him and he would shave by a piece of broken mirror which he kept in his pocket. When he was finished he would leave. This happened quite regularly. I asked my father who he was and he told me it was 'Uncle Bobby'. I never knew an 'Uncle Bobby' so it's quite likely that he was an IRA man on the run – my father would have been a strong IRA sympathiser. It's possible my father was being paid something for providing a safe house, as it were.

One of the best things about moving to the Paddock was the fact that now Daisy came to live with us – Daddy had even built a cowshed for her – so we had fresh milk every morning. That cow was the main source of our diet. The milk was put in a big churn. The cream would settle on the top. When there was nobody watching, my sister Joan would skim all the cream off the milk with a saucer and drink it. We took turns milking the cow. Daisy was very smart; she used to come running if you whistled for her and Paddy or Joan would hold her horns and make believe we were wrestling.

We had no running water, so Timmy used to be sent down to the village pump to fetch water. Mama used to make delicious soda bread with fresh buttermilk; the bread was baked on the hearth in a three-legged oven pot with a lid. You kept putting red turf from the fire under the pot and on top of the lid. It smelt and tasted so good. Our diet largely consisted of bread and milk. We had no hens of our own so sometimes we used to go looking for eggs in hens' nests in the bushes when we went roaming around the fields.

We children all used to sleep in the one bed, which dipped in the middle. We lived and slept in whatever clothes we had on our backs. It was a bit of a squeeze for the six of us but sometimes it was good fun and we would tell each other stories at night to drown out the sound of Mama being shouted at by Daddy. It was comforting in a way being wrapped around each other. But not too pleasant if someone wet the bed! Sometimes you would beg the body sleeping next to you if you could warm your feet on their back; you would promise anything, whether you had it or not.

In general, we used to wash outside and in the winter you might have to crack the ice in the water to wash. On Saturday, which was bath night (so that we would be scrubbed clean for church on Sunday), we used to bring in a tub from the shed and fill it up with water. Sometimes we used to go next door, where there was a well in the yard. They let us take what we needed, throwing in a pail on the end of a rope and pulling it up. We would lift a few buckets home between us before putting the water on the stove to boil. Then we would fill up the tin bath in front of the stove and one by one we would all take our baths, the younger ones sharing. Because we had no washing machine, we used to boil the clothes in a large pot on the fire and then bring them outside, wash them on a scrubbing board and hang them on the hedges to dry.

On Sundays, we'd all march down the road, scrubbed squeaky-clean for church. Mama used to play the church organ and sing at the children's Mass. People used to travel from far and wide just to hear her. We felt very proud of her.

3

To School through the Plains

Maureen, Joan, Dolores, Paddy and I were enrolled in the Curragh National School. I felt terribly grown-up as I set off across the plains of the Curragh. The day we were due to start, my mother took us back to her former home. She wanted my cousin Angela to walk us to school. We left the house with her but I think she ran ahead and left us behind. I suppose she was embarrassed by our ragged clothes.

When I first started school in the Curragh we were still called the 'Yanks'. I suppose we had American accents and were a bit of a novelty at that time. Maureen had a polka-dot scarf which she used to wear to school. The kids used to chase her across the Curragh, teasing her about the 'Yankee scarf' and hitting her with branches of the furze bushes which had thorns on them. I suppose that was the beginning of our feeling 'different' from the other children in the town. We were made to feel like outsiders.

We went to a mixed school, though the boys and girls were separated. A long hall divided the boys' school from the girls'. The school toilets were outside across the schoolyard. A big bell with a handle which stood out on the steps would be rung when school started and finished.

I hated school. I remember being very bad at my lessons. I was always being whacked because of my poor handwriting. The classes were big in those days, with several forms being taught in one classroom. I remember being good at darning and being given the headmaster's socks to darn at home – and that was supposed to be an honour! We were terrified of the teachers; if we were playing on the streets in Brownstown and any of them came through on a walk, we used to run and hide.

When Maureen started school in the Curragh, she was put in the first grade even though she had been in 3B when she was in school in Brooklyn. They said it was because she could not speak Irish. She had to be able to speak Irish to the third-class level before she could be moved up. I guess she was pretty smart because a few months later she was moved up to the third class. She also entered a *feis* that same year in an Irish-speaking contest and was awarded the *fáinne* on 9 May 1937. She never remembers receiving any praise or reward from Mama or Daddy.

Most Fridays in the afternoon the teachers would march those of us who had made our First Communion to confession in the church. The local priest used to visit the classrooms during the religion lessons and you got a tin medal when you got an answer right – I never did.

We had a vice-principal from hell. If you didn't pay attention or spoke out of turn she loved to use a big strap. You had to hold out your hands, palms facing upward, and she would beat the palms with her strap; if you flinched at all you got extra slaps. Then she would wrap that strap around your legs all the way back to your seat. She was a tall, heavy-set woman and her husband was a skinny, henpecked man. He was principal of the boys' school and they had three daughters.

We used to wear in other people's shoes for them. Shoes were made of very hard leather in those days. You'd get awful blisters but it was worth it to get a chance to wear nice new shiny shoes. I had a friend named Noeleen whose shoes I used to break in for her. When I did get shoes of my own they were always hand-me-downs from my sisters and often they'd be full of holes. We were so poor that we used to cut out cardboard to cover the holes in the soles of our shoes. Often in the summer we wouldn't wear shoes at all; I went barefoot most of the time and so did Timmy. Our shoes were generally in such bad shape we kept them just for school.

After school we used to play around the kitchen table. We didn't have any toys at all, so we improvised. We would cut out pictures of women and clothing from advertisements in magazines and newspapers and play a game we called 'Ladies', which involved inventing stories about the women. Kids today just don't use their imagination to the same extent as we used to then. We would spend hours dressing the figures up in paper gowns, changing their outfits and pretending they were going shopping or out to tea parties. We kept our ladies in old cigar boxes, complete with their wardrobes, and had names for every one of them.

When we were able to go to the cinema or picture house, as it was then known, they would always show the

Pathe Gazette Newsreel before the feature film, and there were always items about the British royal family, usually riding in the royal coach pulled by six magnificent white horses. To us it was a fairy-tale world. I was fascinated by the two princesses, Elizabeth and Margaret Rose, and longed more than anything to have a white lace dress like the ones they wore. One day I took down my mother's lace curtains, which had come from her own home, and cut them up, intending to make a lovely lace dress and be like a princess. But the plan was a disaster – there wasn't even enough to make a real dress and my furious mother made me stitch them back together. They never looked the same again, I'm sad to say!

At lunchtime in spring or early autumn, my mother used to bring us on picnics, which we would eat out on the plains of the Curragh where the sheep grazed, the soldiers fought mock wars and the jockeys rode out for their trainers. The smell of the heather was so lovely you just wanted to stay there. One summer, Daddy got us a horse, which he called Maureen Óg. One day while Maureen was riding bareback Daddy put Timmy and me up in front of her. Then he hit the horse hard on its rump and it ran galloping off across the field. Maureen could not hold on to Timmy or me so she threw us off and then stopped the horse. We were both very lucky not to have been badly injured.

One of the great advantages about living in Brownstown was that you could walk over to the racetrack on the Curragh from the town and go right up to the fence across the road from Williams's Corner and watch the races for free. Many's the time Mama and Daddy would bring us out to watch one of the horses they had backed! Half the village would be out, waving their caps and roaring encouragement at the horses and jockeys as they charged past.

One time my father harnessed a jaunting car to a racehorse. The horse bucked and took off at great speed down the main street of Brownstown – people must have thought we were a mad family! I think Joan and myself fell off but my father couldn't stop the horse, so we got left behind and had to walk home.

Once Maureen got the hang of cycling her bike, she taught the rest of us and we would sometimes travel around with three of us on a bike, one on the carrier and one on the saddle (usually Timmy or me because we were small), and Maureen would be stuck standing and pedalling. We all had great fun.

Because there were so few bus routes some people had to cycle from their homes to the nearest bus stop. The bus driver would then throw the bike on top of the bus. Paddy remembers that if you got tired cycling somewhere, you could always get the bus and bring your bike with you. In the summer we used to wander around the village with our pals. The summers were great in those carefree years when Mama was alive. They seemed to go on for ever.

Joan used to visit this couple, Mr and Mrs Ward. He was the town watchmaker and used to teach her how to repair watches. Once, Timmy stole the jam jars Mrs Ward had been storing to use for her homemade gooseberry jam. So she nicknamed him 'Timmy, me jam jars'. Poor

Timmy took them because we no cups or glasses. Joan was at the Wards' one day while Mr Ward was ill in bed. He was taking medicine which made his urine turn blue and he kept the urine in a receptacle on his night table. Unexpectedly some men who had been drinking at Willams's corner pub came by on a visit. The saw the vessel with the blue water in it and asked what it was. Mr Ward was embarrassed and said it was a hair conditioner he was experimenting with. The visitors, of course, wanted to try it and combed the stuff into their hair. They thought it was great. Joan had to leave the house, she was laughing so hysterically.

The biggest business in the town was the corner pub. We called the place Williams's Corner. Even from outside it smelled of stale Guinness, and inside the smell was worse. There was an old woman called Mrs Higgins who lived in the town and was always dressed in black. She used to cross the street every day with her milk cows, always tapping them on the backside with a little stick, putting them out to pasture. She would catch me going by her gate and tell me that she needed her medicine. She would give me a note which I would hand the bartender at the pub. I would then hold my nose until he handed me the 'medicine', which he called her 'baby Powers', in a brown paper bag. When I brought it back to her she would give me a penny. I later discovered that her medicine was whiskey!

Williams's pub had some strange and funny characters. Cotter Brogan was an old guy with a very flat nose. He used to entertain the men by whistling songs through his nose, holding one nostril closed and blowing the sound out through the other. The men used to request songs. I was fascinated watching him while I waited for Mrs Higgins's baby Powers.

Danny Dunne was another town character; he had been in World War I in the Royal Corps of Signals and he had returned home shell-shocked. He wore several overcoats at once, sometimes up to five at one time. They were all in tatters and he never took them off, even in summer. He walked around Brownstown all day, muttering to himself. He looked for cigarette butts on the street and picked them up by sticking a pin in them. Then he would try and smoke them. We kids made up a song about him:

Danny Dunne was a funny old man,
Washed his face in the frying pan,
Combed his hair with the leg of a chair.
Poor old Danny Dunne!

Children can be unthinkingly cruel.

During the day, sometimes I would go to the yard outside the back of the pub, where Jack Ledger would wash out the bottles and pint glasses in a big wooden barrel filled with brown soapy water. I would sit on the ground and help him. He would hand me the glasses after washing them and I would rinse them in another barrel of water and put them upside down on a wooden board. Sometimes we would sing. He liked a song that had a line with the words 'last post and chorus' about a young Irish soldier.

There was a little butcher's shop in Brownstown with an outside counter across from Williams's corner pub. We used to peer in the window and watch the owner cut up the meat, which was always covered in flies. There was always a faithful band of dogs sitting nearby with their tongues hanging out for the few scraps which they would eventually be thrown. The butcher would chop the carcasses in time to his coughs. He always had a cigarette, with an amazing curl of ash, dangling from the corner of his mouth. We used to watch in fascination to see where the ash would fall and wonder who would buy the piece of meat it would end up on. We disguised our laughs as coughs, over the sound of him chopping the meat. He used to wave his cleaver at us and yell, 'Fuck off!' We were full of fun in those days.

Towards the end of the summer, we used to buy a plot in the bog and cut out turf with a *sleán,* which shaped it into blocks. Depending on the weather it took a long time to dry; then was ready to be carted home and stacked outside for fuel for the coming winter.

4
—

MAUREEN HAS A HARD TIME

One day my father told Maureen to go to the store to get
him cigarettes. She was about fourteen years old and had
her hair rolled up in curlers. She wanted to take the
curlers out of her hair before she went to the store but
Daddy would not let her. He told her to hurry but when
she left the house she removed the hideous curlers. When
she came back with the cigarettes my father was furious
when he noticed her curlers were out. So he got a big
shears and grabbed her hair, which was long, and hacked
it off to the scalp. Mama was screaming at him not to do
it but he paid no heed to her. It's almost as if he were
afraid of his daughters growing up.

Once Maureen ditched school and went to the Curragh
races with some of her pals. They call that 'mitching' in
Ireland. Well, who did she bump into at the races but my
father! He sent her home. Later on, when he arrived back
home he was really angry. Maureen started to run away
from him through the fields but he ran after her with a
pitchfork and eventually caught her. He held the pitchfork
over her as he roared at her. Fortunately for her he did

not hit her with it. He ordered Maureen back into the house and with that he gave her 'a kick in the slats'.

When Maureen was only fourteen she graduated with a Leaving Certificate. The day she got her results she was up around the sweet shop. It was dusk and the lights were on in the houses. An apprentice jockey from one of the stud farms was walking by and stopped to say something to her. Suddenly my father appeared out of nowhere and slapped Maureen across the face and roared at her to get home. 'Don't let me ever catch you talking to her again,' he ordered the boy. Maureen was so embarrassed. She ran home, but Daddy chased after her. When he came into the house he warned her to never talk to any of those boys again. She must have felt very brave because she answered him back, 'Why? You were once a jockey boy yourself!' Well that made him livid. He slapped Maureen across the face again, only this time it knocked her unconscious. Mama screamed at him to get out. Daddy pushed her into the corner. Maureen came to after Dad poured a bucket of water over her.

It was around then that Daddy must have started planning to put Maureen in the convent. Not long afterwards, towards the end of 1938, he brought her to Naas one day and left her with the Sisters of Mercy. He wanted her locked away from the world. Maureen was lonely and miserable. So one night she bravely decided to run home. Given the welcome she was likely to receive from my father, the convent must have been pretty awful. She had some money given to her by Uncle Pat, who had a shoe-repair shop across the street from the convent. She knew what time the bus from Naas departed for Brownstown.

So she climbed over the wall while all the girls were in bed and ran across to the bus stop. All the time she stood waiting for the bus she was terrified that the nuns would arrive to drag her back. But the bus arrived promptly and she quickly jumped onto it. She felt sick at the thought of Daddy's reaction.

It was night when Maureen arrived back at our house. She went to the window and looked into the kitchen. To Maureen's relief, Mama was there on her own sewing by the fire and there was no sign of my father. When she went into the house Mama said, 'What are you doing here? What is your father going to say?' Well as you can imagine, he had plenty to say. Maureen was black and blue for days.

Small wonder she felt rejected at home. Unknown to her, Daddy was planning to send her away to another convent. Neither he nor Mama gave her the slightest hint of what was going to happen. On St Stephen's Day 1938, Daddy burst into our bedroom and shook her awake. He told her that she was going on a trip with him. Poor Maureen had no idea what lay ahead of her. She quickly got dressed and had some breakfast. She felt a sudden dread when he told her to say goodbye to Mama, who was out in the back of the house. Mama was crying but Maureen had no idea why. I sometimes wonder if Mama had an inkling of how ill she was at that point, for that was to be the last time Maureen would set eyes upon her. I guess Mama was too afraid to stand up to Daddy. The rest of us didn't really pay much heed to Maureen's departure because as far as we were concerned they were setting off on a day trip. I mean it wasn't as if she even had any luggage. We were busy playing with our new Christmas kitten around the fire.

Maureen doesn't recall how they got to the station but clearly remembers being on the train and Daddy telling her to count the telephone poles as they went along. From the station, they got a taxi because there were very few buses in operation over the Christmas holidays. Their final destination was the Good Shepherd Convent in Limerick. Poor Maureen's heart sank when she saw where she was. She felt desperately deceived and rejected. Maureen and Daddy were brought into the parlour and while they were there he warned her that if she so much as attempted to run off he would slay her. 'Daddy, please don't leave me here,' she pleaded. And with that he walked out the door and she was abandoned again.

The nun returned and asked Maureen if she knew why her father had put her in the convent. When she said she did not she was told it was because her father was afraid that she 'would become a mother'. It was his way of saying that she might get pregnant. Up to that point the only boys she had ever talked to were those jockey boys, in the presence of her father.

The mother superior said that Maureen would have to be given a new name, a saint's name, and since she was from Kildare her name would be Bridie, a variation of Brigid, the patron saint of Kildare. She never knew why all the girls' names were changed but she was Bridie all the time she was there. No two girls had the same name. Whenever a girl left, the name that she had been called was available for the next girl who came into the convent. It was almost as if the inmates had no identity.

They rose every morning at five o'clock, got dressed, washed their face and hands and went down to Mass in the convent chapel. From the day she entered the convent on 26 December 1938 until September 1939 she was never outside the convent grounds, which were surrounded by a tall wall. She could not see over it but sometimes when she was in the bathroom and looked out the window she could hear and see people on the street. She used to listen to their conversations for a hint of normality. She never had a visitor the entire time she was there.

The convent had a big commercial laundry and did the cleaning for most of Limerick city. Initially Maureen was assigned to the ironing room and got burnt quite often from the irons. After some time there she was moved to the lace-making room, which she liked. It was less noisy and steamy than the big laundry and also more creative. The nuns taught her how to make Limerick lace. It was sold to people who came to visit the convent, which was well known as the place to get the lace. I think they were the only people who made it. The lace was very delicate and quite expensive. Tourists used to come to see it and they would be given a tour of the lace-making room.

The girls wore a uniform consisting of a navy dress, black shoes and stockings and a white, starched collar. If they broke any of the rules the collar would be taken away from them and everybody would know they were being punished. It was a mark of shame to be without the collar. I don't think Maureen ever lost hers but she was constantly in fear of losing it. Infractions of rules might be just minor incidents such as talking when the girls were supposed to be silent. They all slept in a long dormitory with only one bathroom at the end. Up till then Maureen still used to wet her bed occasionally. So all she could think about every night was whether she would make it to the bathroom on time.

5

MAMA'S DEATH

I will always remember that morning of Sunday 30 July 1939. Mama had gone out to milk the cow, I was helping Dolores knead the dough for bread in the kitchen, Paddy and Joan were hanging out washing and Timmy had gone off to the water pump.

After my mother had finished the milking, I heard the kitchen door creaking open. I looked up from my baking to see Mama stumble in the door and collapse. She lay in a crumpled heap on the floor beside her upturned pail of milk. My sisters and I helped her to a chair but she just sat there staring ahead blankly without uttering a word. My sister Paddy ran across the street for help to a neighbour who had a car. We all helped my mother into the car and Paddy went off with her to the Kildare Infirmary a few miles away. I had this awful feeling in the pit of my stomach that she was never going to return.

When Paddy and Daddy arrived home that night, we knew by Paddy's tear-stained face that something awful had happened. Daddy announced to us brusquely, 'Your mother won't be coming home; she died tonight.' Then he went out the door. There was no one to comfort us. We just clung to each other in shock, half-comprehending his words.

Poor Mama died upon arrival at the hospital – of kidney failure. In those days they didn't have dialysis. She'd probably had a kidney problem for years and didn't know it. Anyway, after having all those children, she would have been tired a lot of the time. She was anointed by a priest while Paddy held a candle over her forehead. Then Paddy kissed her goodbye and they moved her down to the mortuary in the hospital. Apparently, Daddy arrived a few hours later. It had been hard to trace his whereabouts because of the occasional nature of his work at that time.

Later I told my sisters about my visit to the sweet shop the day before and began to get very worried. While I was waiting, one of the shopkeepers was talking to a man whose wife had just died. I had been unintentionally listening to their conversation, but I was slapped across the face for staring at a recently widowed man. So naturally I assumed it was all my fault that Mama had died because I had been looking at the widower. Paddy held me in her arms despite her own tears, and Joan and Dolores told me not to be silly.

The last letter Maureen received from Mama was written the day before she died. In it Mama told her that she was going to leave Daddy. She asked Maureen to remember that she had always tried to bring us up as good Catholics. I remember my father often being angry with my mother. There must have been times when they were under unbearable pressure with the worry of no work and six mouths to feed. I'm sure she must have blamed him in some respects for all he had taken her away from. I remember hearing my parents fighting and always in the back of my mind I can hear her crying. Now I wonder how she put up with her misery for so long; I suppose she felt she couldn't leave us. However, poor Mama died, so she never got a chance to leave and find peace and happiness. It was very sad. She never got a second chance.

Maureen still remembers being called to the mother superior's office to be told about Mama's death. There was a rule that when you were called into this little room you had to kneel down by her desk. Showing very little emotion she told Maureen that she had some bad news for her. Maureen immediately presumed that something had happened to our sister Dolores because she had been ill in a hospital in Dublin. She soon realised that it was not Dolores but her mother that something had happened to but there were no words of comfort or consolation. She was merely told she did not have to go back to the lace-making room that day. Instead, she was instructed to go to the chapel and pray. She was also informed that her father did not want her to go home for the funeral. Evidently he said he had enough children at home. After Maureen had gone to the chapel to pray she went upstairs to the dorm and just lay down on her bed for the rest of the day. It was inhumane the way she was treated.

The next day it was business as usual. Being away from home when Mama died, Maureen did not realise the full impact of our mother's death until much later. After all she had not seen her for several months. Maureen had become used to being away from her. She really could not comprehend what being without her was like.

Meanwhile at Brownstown Daddy decided to send Timmy and me to Naas to tell our grandmother and his family what had happened to Mama. He put us on a bus and told the driver to be sure and let us off at the first row of houses as you entered Naas. On the way the driver stopped in a town called Newbridge, about halfway to Naas. He took pity on Timmy and me and bought us ice creams. One thing I can't understand was why our father sent us children with the news. Maybe it was to get us out of the way of funeral arrangements and keep us occupied.

When we arrived at Granny's in Naas we told them the awful news. Granny looked at me angrily. Then she hit me across the face for telling fibs. Timmy yelled, 'But it's true! It's true!' Then we both started bawling. With that, Granny blessed herself and said, 'Jesus, Mary and Joseph, what's to become of you!' Aunt Lillie threw her arms around us and cried. Granny decided to accompany us back on the bus for the funeral. She had never been on a bus or a car in her life and she was terrified. We had to hold her hand all the way to Brownstown.

As is the custom in Ireland, they held a wake the next day for her and the funeral on the following day. The day of the funeral it was raining very hard. Timmy, Joan and I were not allowed to go to the funeral. We waited at the bedroom window with our grandmother and watched as the funeral procession passed by. An open hearse pulled by two horses carried the coffin and it stopped for a moment outside our house. Granny told us to say a prayer but we were crying so hard we couldn't. Then the realisation hit us that we would never hear her voice or see her again.

The local newspaper carried the following account:

Sincere regret was occasioned in the Curragh area by the death of Mrs Violet C. Connolly, Brownstown, wife of Mr Timothy Connolly, Brownstown, which took place at the Kildare Infirmary on Sunday last, 30 July. Deceased was the daughter of the late Mr William Thornton, who, some years ago, was the popular proprietor of a large general-stores business at the Curragh Camp. Death came to Mrs Connolly with tragic suddenness. She was a valued member of the choir of St Brigid's (Garrison) Church, Curragh Camp, and on Sunday last was in her usual place at Mass. In the evening, she was suddenly taken ill and was conveyed to Kildare Infirmary, where she passed away soon after admittance. Deceased leaves a youthful family to mourn her loss and the deep sympathy of the Curragh community is with them and the bereaved husband, Mr Tim Connolly, who is well known in Irish racing circles.

The remains were removed from the Kildare Infirmary to Suncroft Parish Church on Monday evening, there being a large attendance of friends and sympathisers. Following 8 o'clock Mass (celebrated by Very Rev M. Brophy, PP) on Tuesday, the funeral took place to Carna Cemetery, the cortège being large and representative and including the members of St Brigid's (Garrison) Church choir.

The chief mourners were Timothy Connolly

(husband), Dolores and Patricia (daughters), William Thornton (brother), Mrs Sylvester, Mrs R. Black, Miss Claire Black, B. Barry, R. Black, Victor Black (relatives).

She was buried in Suncroft, where little Victor was also buried. Dolores and Paddy said they took up his coffin and put down our Mama's first and then put his on top of hers. Mama's death marked the end of our childhood.

The cemetery was not far away from our house and Timmy and myself would often walk there and play hide-and-seek among the gravestones. The cemetery was surrounded by a four-foot wall made of fieldstones, which were common in the countryside. We would get up on the wall and walk around on it. Sometimes I would run behind a high gravestone and Timmy would look for me. One time when he could not find me I jumped out from behind a headstone and scared him, making him cry. We used to pick cowslips and put them on Mama's grave. Death became a part of our daily little lives.

After Mama died, life with our father was hell. We had neither food nor clothes. We had nothing, and on top of that, we were beaten. He would look at us and say, 'I should have raised cattle instead.' He just could not cope. Timmy and I would go knocking on doors asking for food. Sometimes we could smell bacon frying and it would drive us crazy. There were times when someone would give us a piece of a stale end of bread, which we were happy to get. Our father worked far away from our home and only came home on weekends and then he tended to disappear on binges. So we mostly had to fend for ourselves. When we were together, we used to think we would report him for physical abuse and then we thought we would all be put in an orphanage if we did that; worst of all, we would probably end up being separated from one another.

Once when we didn't have any firewood left and the cold became too much to stand any longer we started removing the inside panels from Daisy's cowshed. When we pulled the first board out rats as big as cats ran out, so we told our friend and neighbour Maurice and he brought a ferret and some men with big clubs and pitchforks. Timmy, Joan and I got on the roof to watch. The men waited outside and Maurice put the ferret down between the boards. Suddenly rats were running in all directions, being clubbed to death and stabbed with pitchforks by the men outside. There were blood and guts everywhere. When my father came home we were about to take boards from the cowshed roof for firewood but he caught us just in time and made us go out into the fields to find firewood. We had burnt everything and anything, even furniture, to make heat. It was hard work carrying it home, since most of it was heavy boughs from trees broken off in storms. When I look back on this period, I'm conscious of how many decisions were left to us as children. We were totally neglected.

We were pretty much on our own. We played games that were sometimes very dangerous. We decided one day to play cowboys and Indians. Our sister Paddy was the hostage. We tied her to a chair and ran around her with lighted newspapers, chanting Indian sounds. Her dress caught fire and we had to put out the flames. She was

OK but we never played that game again. Nobody wanted to be the hostage.

One day while playing on the roof of the cowshed I accidentally pushed Timmy off. He suffered such a shock that he lost his voice for days. I was hoping he wouldn't get it back too soon or he might tell on me. It was awful; I was so scared. My father didn't know what was wrong with him and I was too scared to explain that I had pushed him off the cowshed. And fortunately Timmy couldn't tell him – and never did!

Once Paddy spilled a pan of boiling grease while she was frying bread for us. The fat went all over her thighs and the burns were so bad she would stay up all night moaning, crying and beating the bed. Mr Quirk across the road thought it was a cow in distress. Daddy wasn't at home at the time and we didn't know how to help her – the pain must have been terrible for her. Eventually her wounds healed in time but she was left with terrible scars and when she wore a bathing costume in later years she had to wear one that covered the tops of her thighs.

My days at school were few and far between after Mama died. My father was never around and I never knew my lessons. So the teacher was always whacking me with the big black strap, which she kept attached to her belt. Timmy was getting the same from his schoolmaster, along with threats of skinning him alive and hanging him by his wrists. One day Timmy couldn't take it any more and he ran away. He went missing for three days. He had walked to Dublin, forty miles away, and had no soles left on his shoes. He was eight years old at the time. We did not know what had happened to him. There was a place near us called the Sewerage Farm. It was surrounded by a high wall. Someone told us that they had seen Timmy walking on the wall. It was thought that perhaps he had fallen in.

I went over there a few times a day and called out, 'Timmy, please come home; Daddy won't beat you.' Fortunately the police in Dublin found him. He had been reported to them because he had been riding up and down the elevator of Clery's department store the whole day. He told me he had a great time. Everybody was feeding him cake, cookies and lemonade. I was so happy to see him that I started crying.

Timmy was deathly afraid of storms, so whenever there was thunder and lightning, no matter where he was he would come running home, screaming at the top of his voice all the way, 'Open the door! Open the door!' Then he would just run right in and hide under the table. Paddy and I were also afraid so we used to hide in the bedroom, but my daddy said it didn't matter where you were if it's going to hit you. So we never hid again and got over our fear.

Father Brophy, with his big fat belly, used to come to our school and ask us religious questions. If you gave the right answer he would give you a medal of the Virgin Mary. I never got one. When Mama died he never came to us to see if there was anything that could be done to help us. I wondered in later years if this was because he was a bit afraid of our father. Or maybe he just didn't care. It hurt that in spite of the contribution my mother had made to his church nobody made any effort to protect us kids.

6

A Motherless Family

Timmy and I loved to sing. Timmy had a beautiful voice. We would sing in our neighbour's kitchen and be rewarded with a piece of bread with country butter and lumps of crystal sugar. Just after Mama died there was a singing contest in the old picture house on the Curragh. The night of the singing contest Timmy sang a song called 'Mother' and I sang 'When I Grow Too Old to Dream'. I had practised with a scratchy old Gracie Fields record. I loved the song and played it all the time. Timmy was the first to sing:

M is for the million things she gave me.
O is only that she's growing old.
T is for the tears she shed to save me.
H is for her heart that's made of gold.
E is for her eyes with love-light shining.
R is right and right she'll always be.
Put them all together, they spell Mother,
A word that means the world to me.
She'll cry for you, sigh for you,

Yes even die for you:
That's what God made mothers for.

Everyone in the picture house knew our mother had just died. There was not a dry eye in the place. People were hanging over the balcony applauding. Timmy won the first prize. It was a silver-plated cup. I won second prize of a box of melted sweets. We ate them on the way home.

The cinema was owned by my Aunt Madge's sister, Mrs Sylvester. We had no radio, unlike other houses, and the only entertainment we had was this movie house in the camp. None of the Sylvesters ever spoke to us. They would walk past us as if they did not know us. Of course we never had money for the movies. Sometimes friends of ours, Claire and Vi Black, who sold the tickets, would let us sneak in without paying. The cinema opened up a whole new world to us. It offered us an escape from our sad little lives. Cocooned inside the warmth we were carefree kids again.

I loved movies with Shirley Temple and Roy Rogers. I had a crush on Roy Rogers. I knew all his songs by heart. Sometimes, I would play at being Shirley Temple and put on a show for the kids. There was a girl in school who looked like her. She had big ringlets and nice clothes but she was missing one eye. Her mother would make one big ringlet that covered the missing eye. She was a Protestant so when we had prayers the teacher would send her out into the hallway.

We also loved Western films – with Roy Rogers, Gene Autry and Tom Mix. We also loved horror movies like *Frankenstein* and *Dracula*. But most of all, we loved musicals with Shirley Temple, Deanna Durbin, Kathryn Grayson, Nelson Eddy and Jeanette MacDonald. I still keep their tapes in my car. I vowed then to become a movie star. And this was the cinema where it all began.

When we went to the movies I couldn't get close enough to the screen, so Joan and I would sit in the very first row, where we felt close enough to the stars to touch them. I used to drive Joan crazy by always asking her what was going to happen next. She would snap, 'Why don't you ask them?' and that would temporarily shut me up.

One day, when we were in school, a captain from the military camp invited anyone who wanted to come after school to the mess hall, where there was always leftover bread and tea. Timmy, Joan and I went along with some other kids whom we didn't know. There was a big fat woman behind the counter who looked and acted like a matron from a prison. She used to pile up plates full of stale, almost musty heels of bread, with a scrape of jam. Sometimes the piles were so unbalanced that they fell on to the floor but we ate it anyway, under her baleful eye. It was made very plain to us that she did not want us there.

The captain also told us that the school could use the pool at the military camp once a week. None of us knew how to swim but in great excitement I borrowed a rubber bathing suit for the adventure. I almost drowned. It was my first time in a pool. When I went into the water the heavy rubber bathing dress filled up with water and pulled me under. Struggling for air, I managed to climb out of the pool, gushing water like a fountain and so embarrassed by the general laughter that I vowed to myself never to return. Joan was very upset because she had been afraid I might drown.

After Mama died, Maureen began to feel more secure in the convent than she had ever done at home. I think it was a refuge for her. Life was so peaceful there. After a time she thought she wanted to become a nun. A few weeks later, the mother superior, whose name was Mother Ignatius, asked Maureen if she still wanted to enter a convent and she said that she did. So plans were made for her to go to the Convent of Franciscan Missionaries of Mary in Loughglynn, County Roscommon, in September 1939.

Maureen, at only fifteen and a half, was too young to be a postulant. For the moment she had to continue with her studies and learn Latin. This community of nuns had a farm and all the sisters worked in one job or the another. They made cheese, which was sold to stores. Maureen never had to do any work except study and keep her room clean. She was allowed to roam around the farm and learned a little French from the nuns, who were mostly Belgian. There was a lake near the convent and in the winter, when it became frozen, the nuns would skate in their wooden clogs.

She asked if she could go home at Christmas as she had not seen any of her family for over a year. It was agreed that she should go home and return after Christmas. She doesn't recall anything of the visit home and returned to the convent as planned but it was never the same for her again. Maybe the visit home brought her back in touch with the reality of Mama's death and her emotions. It probably helped her confront her grief.

In May 1940 she left the convent. Daddy made her life a misery when she returned home, but she loved being with her sisters and brother again. Daddy arranged for her to work in a large house in Ballymany, where she took care of some children and served meals. But this was not for her. Nor would it have been what Mama wanted for her. Maureen was bright and intelligent and wanted to do something more with her life.

One day, Maureen went to Naas to see a travelling show. She had always been told that she had a good singing voice. The show was leaving Naas the following day for Cork city. What did Maureen do only follow them! She was young and naive, and sure that they would let her join up with their troupe. However, when she got to Cork and told them her plans, they told her that she had to get back home before the police came and they got into trouble.

So there she was in Cork all alone and afraid to go home. She was sure that Daddy would do something terrible to her. She needed security and somebody to care for her. So she went to the Good Shepherd convent in Cork and asked them if they would contact Mother Ignatius in Limerick and see if she could go back there. Maureen was sure the mother superior was very disappointed about her not becoming a Franciscan nun in the convent in Roscommon. It was agreed that she could return; so back she went. But after some time there she was miserable again. She was floundering with no direction in her life and nobody to help her. She needed a mother or father to help her.

In the Good Shepherd convent, no talking was allowed,

with the exception of recreation times. Meals were taken in silence in a large refectory. One of the nuns would read to the others during the meals. Some girls were assigned to the kitchen and they set the tables, served the meals and cleaned up afterwards. On Fridays and Saturdays they were forced to drink Epsom salts. There would be a big tub of it and they had to line up and take a cup of it. The girls used to try and hide but the nuns would always know that they had not been in the line to get it and they would come looking for them. This was their way of making sure the girls' bowels were purged at least once a week.

Maureen had friends there with whom she used to take walks around the grounds. She was always talking to them about the outside world. This was against the rules: they were supposed to forget the world outside, do their work and pray. Maureen had been warned not to mention it. But I guess it was impossible for her and she was sent home again to her father. By this time she was nearly seventeen years old.

Maureen did not even dare to think of what was going to happen to her when she got home. When she arrived at the train station in Kildare she used the few shillings given to her by the nuns to go to Newbridge and find a room to rent. The room she found was apart from the main house but she had only been there one day and night when there was a knock on her bedroom door. She opened it only to face a policeman. He said that my father told him that she was to be put out of the room and sent home. She was terrified and went home immediately. She does not remember what occurred with her father when she got there but she stayed at home for another six months.

She and Paddy used to fight all the time. Maureen made her own clothes by hand and Maurice Condron, who had got rid of the rats for us, and about whom I shall tell you more later, used to give her the odd shilling every now and again for doing errands for him. She would use that money to buy fabric to make a dress. The result was that Paddy always wanted to wear Maureen's clothes and Maureen did not want that. So they fought. Once she had made a nice dress and Paddy wanted to wear it to go to a dance before Maureen had ever worn it. Maureen said no. Daddy was out in the back of the house burning some leaves and he heard them fighting. He came into the house to find out what all the shouting was about and when Maureen told him he said, 'I can solve that problem.' And with that he grabbed the dress and took it out the back, where he was burning leaves, and threw it into the fire. 'There, that takes care of that argument,' he said spitefully.

When the tinkers came through the town in their colourful caravans they used to pile clothes on the street for sale. One time I saw a yellow dress that I wanted. I showed them my penny. The old tinker woman glared at me first, then nodded that I could have the dress. I grabbed it and raced home. I washed it carefully by hand and hung it out on the fence to dry. During the night a big windstorm came up. The next morning I went out to get my dress and there it was in shreds around the wire fence. I cried all day for my little yellow dress. Years later, when I earned my first wage packet, I went out and bought myself a yellow dress.

Old Maurice Condron was a big-framed man with snow-white hair. He was kind and fatherly and lived in a little one-roomed, white-washed cottage. The room had a big hearth in which he always had a big roaring fire going. He loved poetry and I would ask him to recite for me. My favourite was 'The Harper and His Dog' by Thomas Campbell (1774–1844):

When the night was so dark, and the night was so
cold
And Pat and his dog were grown weary and old,
How snugly we slept in my old coat of grey,
And he licked me for kindness, my poor dog Tray.

Though my wallet was scant, I remembered his case
Nor refused my last crust to his pitiful face;
But he died at my feet on a cold winter's day
And I played a lament for my poor dog Tray.

Timmy used to accompany Maurice on his cart. He had a big tank pulled by a big old dray horse named Grakel which was useful in his business of emptying the out-houses in town. He would let us hop up on the tank and take a ride with him while he did his job. It smelt really bad but Maurice smoked a pipe and most of the time all you could smell was the tobacco. When Grakel was unharnessed we use to play on him, sliding down his back and hanging on to his neck. He was a very gentle horse, never moving as we played with him.

Maurice would give me a penny to make his bed and clean out the ashes from the hearth. He had pet names for all of us: Maureen was 'Maureen O'Sullivan', Joan 'Sally was the weasel', Dolores 'Kitty Cut a Dash up the Mountain'. He used to nickname me 'Mary Theresa Coalbox' because of my dark hair.

One day when Timmy was riding with Maurice on his float, the horse jerked and Timmy fell backwards into the container, which was full to the brim with raw sewage. Maurice hauled him out and rolled him over and over again in the grass before throwing buckets of water over him. No one wanted to be near Timmy for days and I don't think the smell ever came out of his suit – and it was the only one he had. Timmy was upset because, as he quite rightly said, everyone was running away from him.

Unfortunately, Maurice got sick and died very suddenly. We were devastated because he had been like a father figure to us for a while and his death came so close after Mama's. The townspeople held a wake for him in his own house. He was laid out on his bed and all the people were going in to see him. My father told me to go in to see Maurice but I wouldn't, so he took me by the arm and tried to force me through the door. I put my arms out and kept them rigid so he couldn't push me in. Finally he let me go and I ran away from him. I always missed Maurice and his poetry.

Timmy and I were so young when our mother died that we seriously lacked the emotional support that children look to their parents for. However, we didn't know otherwise and we were lucky enough to have Paddy, Maureen, Joan and Dolores. We were all very close as a result, all struggling simply to survive. But children need to grow up feeling loved and secure. We never did. In those days, children were often considered to be in the way of adults, whereas today's children are tolerated and indulged. Our father was very irresponsible towards us but even though he wasn't a very caring or paternal father, and even though he drank and was violent, he was still our father. Children tend to be all-forgiving; we sort of accepted our father, as children do. Even the children of murderers get upset when their daddies go to jail. But although there was a kind of attachment to our father we were always happiest when he was away.

7
—

OLIVER TWIST HAD IT GOOD!

There were times we were so hungry we would eat raw turnips and crab apples from someone else's fields. We used to go out into the fields looking for blackberries and mushrooms. We would pull turnips and sit and eat them dirty and raw. Once a bull chased us and we just about made it over the hedge. Another time we climbed over a wall of an estate near us into an orchard of apples. The caretaker saw us and started yelling and shaking his cane at us but we did not run away. We told him we were starving. He used his cane to pull down a bough heavy with apples, which was kind of him. He shook the bough and the apples started to fall to the ground. One fell and hit him on the nose and caused it to start bleeding. This made him angry so we scooped up the apples and started running. He was yelling as we scrambled back over the wall, almost dropping our catch. They were the best apples we ever had.

We would go out early in the morning to look for mushrooms in the fields; you could always get as many as you wanted. We would pull a long blade of grass and knot one end of it. Then we would slip the blade of grass through the stalk of any mushrooms we found and carry them side by side until we got home. We seemed to know instinctively which mushrooms were the right ones to pick. When we got home we would fry them in some lard and gobble them up straight away. I don't know how we knew which varieties were safe and which ones should not be eaten. And then of course we used to work at the bog, cutting turf.

After blackberry-picking we would eat them with a little sugar and cream; they were very tasty. We still had milk from Daisy and some eggs found in bushes when hens laid 'away'. Paddy remembers planting potatoes in the back garden and covering them with straw and dirt so as to preserve them for the winter. Whenever you needed some you dug them out. We did the same with apples, except we put them in barrels.

At one stage Timmy was eating anything he could find, from the plaster to newspapers. Then he started eating a piece of his jacket one thread at a time; my father whipped him for doing it.

We used to go to all the wakes in our town. We knew that you always got a piece of cake after you said a prayer. Timmy, Joan and I went to old Johnny Quirk's wake; he was laid out on his bed in a white shroud. We knelt down beside the bed and, as we did, a large bluebottle landed on his nose. We were fascinated watching this great big fly walking up and down on this dead man's bony nose. Timmy looked at me and twitched his nose. We started laughing. We were almost denied our piece of cake that night. We were quickly ushered out the door. Fortunately Timmy had already stuffed his pockets with food.

Somewhere in my memory I can see Uncle Thomas in the house. I can remember slicing a piece of bread for him and his complaining about how thin it was cut. I think he came back from America and stayed with us until he went to a retirement home in Dublin, where he later died. He had a pension from the job he had worked at for years in Brooklyn. Mama was always very good to him when she was alive because of his kindness to her when she arrived in America.

Paddy got a job cleaning for three little old ladies, one of whom was in a wheelchair. Two of them were like the pair in the movie *Arsenic and Old Lace.* Paddy would be scrubbing the floors and they'd walk by and pray. They told her that if she passed by anyone working she had to say, 'God bless the work.' The one who was in the wheelchair told Paddy that when she died everything she had would go to her, but Paddy didn't know that a will had to be formalised and witnessed in writing, so that when the old lady died the only thing Paddy got her were her false teeth which she had removed and brought home when she was dying. We all used to play with them, forcing them into our mouths and pretending we were Dracula. Paddy had to wash and dress the old woman and plug up her nose for the wake, all at the age of fifteen.

Gradually, after Mother died, our whole family unit seemed to split apart. After a few years Dolores and Joan went to work for families in Dublin and Paddy worked for Aunt Madge for a short time, and a small salary. Aunt Madge was very nice to her. She taught her light-hearted little songs and if she had a date she would wait up for her. Eventually, Paddy went to Dublin to work at a boarding house for people coming off the boat from England.

Things continued to be very bad at home. Father was violent towards us all but Maureen got the worst of it. This was awful for us to watch because Maureen was so good to us. She was a sort of mother figure to us all after Mama died. My sister Dolores had to have her hair shaved off because she had open sores all over her head. My sister Joan lost all her hair too. When it started to fall out, Maureen made up her mind to take her to the dispensary in Kilcullen; so she put her on the bicycle carrier and rode all the way to the doctor in the bitter cold. It was a hilly trip as well, so at times they both had to get off and walk the bike. From the dispensary Joan was sent to the Naas hospital, where they immediately put her in a bath and scrubbed her clean – she was their 'little pigeon' because she was so small. Then they told her they were sending her to a Dublin hospital. One of the patients asked her which hospital it was and she said it was the 'Whore Hospital', whereupon the patient nearly fell out of the bed laughing. Joan had completely misheard the name of the hospital, which was Hume St Hospital, and had no comprehension of what a whore was.

When her hair finally grew back it was almost all grey and curly. This was caused by stress and shock, as she was only twelve years old. While she was in the hospital the Germans bombed Dublin in error. Everybody at the hospital had to be taken down to the basement for safety. Sometimes we could hear the planes returning home after dropping bombs in England.

When war was declared between England and Germany some of the German boats sank off the coast of Ireland and some of the bombers crashed coming back from the raids on England. Since Ireland was a neutral country those sailors and airmen were not considered prisoners of war. They were called internees and were treated quite well. They had to report back to the internment camp on the Curragh only by a certain time at night. They became friendly with the Irish people and made toys for the children at Christmas.

Brownstown had a big military camp. During the war you had to have a pass to go through the camp. There used to be a sentry in a little wooden hut and he would say, 'Who goes there?' and you had to answer, 'Friend.' Then he would say, 'Advance one at a time.' The military police were known as Redcaps. We became friendly with some of the Germans, getting to know them when they were out on their walks through the village. A group of them regularly used to march up and down past my Uncle Billy's house, singing German songs; an Alsatian dog, a pet, I suppose, walked with them. I became friendly in particular with a boy called Otto Bruch. He was still a kid and very short, with freckles and red hair, and he seemed more like a little boy than a soldier. He loved animals and so did I and he had a little Jack Russell in the camp.

Otto was very sweet and very kind. He gave me a pet goat that used to try and follow me to school so that I would have to chase it back home. One day when I came home from school, my father had made a big stew. After we had finished eating, I went out to look for my goat but it was gone. I asked my father where it was. He answered, 'What do you think you just ate.' I felt sick and I wished my father was dead. My sister Joan says she heard the goat scream as my father cut its throat. She also said that after he had done it he came into the house and said, 'That sounded like a real baby's scream.' We all had horrific nightmares for ages after that. He really had no idea how to bring up children nor did he seem to realise the impact of his actions. He seemed mentally disconnected at times and was such a destructive force in our life. He destroyed everything good we ever had. We hated him because of the way he treated us and we were always terrified of him.

Paddy made friends with a German named Hans Gobel and he used to carry her over his shoulders like a sack of potatoes. He taught her some German. Paddy recalls that he asked Daddy's permission to marry her and promised her that he would become a Catholic. But my father said she was too young; she was only sixteen years old. She missed him when the war was over and he had to go back to Germany. She was also friendly with Kurt and Werner. Kurt sometimes used to accompany Maureen while she was out walking but she never really knew any of the internees very well. She was not interested in them.

Maureen decided she wanted to become a nurse and left for London in September 1941. She was seventeen and a half years of age and was going to work in a private psychiatric hospital. When she arrived in London she took the Tube to the station nearest to the hospital and while she was walking from the station to the hospital she heard a siren sounding and suddenly everyone in the street started running. Maureen did not know what was happening. Then suddenly there was an enormous explosion and a bomb exploded in the next block to her. The impact of the bomb lifted her off the ground. She was taken to casualty, where she was treated for shock, but she was sufficiently recovered to start work at the psychiatric hospital the next day.

There was no provision for classroom studies; it was all on-the-job training. Maureen fitted in and adapted very quickly. She stayed at that hospital for a few months and then heard about what were called cooperative nurses. These were untrained nurses like herself who joined a central pool and were sent to hospitals that were seriously understaffed due to many nurses serving in the armed services. The pay was better and there was more freedom. By now she was eighteen years old and since she was a good dancer she loved going out to lots of dances, especially those held in Covent Garden Opera House, which was used as a dance hall during the war. There she met a young woman called Annie, with whom she became very friendly, and they spent their time off together. Annie was divorced and had a young son who, along with many other London children, had been evacuated away from the bombings to the safety of the country.

The US entered the war after Pearl Harbour and the first American troops landed in England in the spring of 1942. Annie and Maureen continued to go to the dances together and at times they were invited to dances at some of the American bases. Maureen met two men at these dances. One was a Canadian named Lorne. He was married and had been a schoolteacher in Canada. The other was an American colonel in the Air Corps. His name was Sammy Mariello and he was from Long Island. He had originally been with the Flying Tigers in China and then with the Eagle Squadron of the RAF, and now that the US was in the war he was in the American air corps. Maureen always assured us that some day she was going to go back to America. Little did she know how soon it would happen. Maureen was never bashful about going after what she wanted, and it was the best lesson in life she ever taught me.

That year Mrs Eleanor Roosevelt, the president's wife, came to London. She travelled widely overseas during the war. Maureen decided to write her a letter telling her that she was an American citizen and wanted to go back to America. Not long afterwards, she received a notice from the US embassy asking her to report to them. She was told that Mrs Roosevelt had instructed them to make arrangements for her to go back to the US. As an American citizen in a country at war, Maureen was entitled to be repatriated. She was asked if she would accompany three underage children home to New York. Their parents were working for the Red Cross in London and she was told that she would get $50 when she delivered them to their grandparents on Park Avenue in New York. Maureen was so excited to be going to America. The American consul told her that she would have to get a copy of her parents' marriage certificate before she could be issued with an American passport. In later years, we often wondered why this was necessary. After all, she had an American birth certificate.

It meant that Maureen had to write to her father and

he replied that he wanted her to come home to fetch it. Maureen refused because she was afraid that he would not let her go back. In the end she received it by post and when she read it she knew why he had wanted to talk to her. The marriage certificate showed the date of marriage as April 1924, which was four months after Maureen's birth. When she returned to the embassy with the certificate she was told that she would have to renounce her Irish citizenship through her parents and reaffirm her US citizenship. The embassy official also told her to be prepared to leave at a moment's notice and not to talk to anyone about it. In the meantime she left her job and stayed with her friend Annie in London.

A few months later Timmy and I got a letter with an American postmark telling us that she had arrived in New York. Apparently her departure had been as sudden as predicted. One day a telegram arrived telling her to report to the embassy with her belongings immediately. She gathered what few things she had and left at once, taking the Underground to the embassy, where she met her three charges for the first time.

They were put on a train for Scotland which steamed right up to the dock. When they arrived, Maureen noticed that there were a lot of servicemen around. The Red Cross workers came over and looked after her and the children. Apparently, the famous liner the *Queen Elizabeth*, which was moored off the coast, had been converted into a troopship for the duration of the war. They were taken out to it by a smaller boat. While on the dock, who did Maureen bump into but her Canadian dancing partners, Sammy Mariello and Lorne Webber. They were being sent home. Sammy was not injured but poor Lorne had lost both his hands when a grenade that he had been carrying had exploded.

Maureen and the children were given a cabin in the first-class section. However, the cabin had been stripped of all the luxurious fittings and instead it had bunks built into it. All Maureen remembers of the voyage was being seasick the entire five days. Sammy used to force her to walk up and down the deck, telling her that it would make her feel better. Someone offered her a bottle of Coca-Cola on one occasion but she hadn't a clue what it was. They were told that they had been followed by a U-boat all the way across the Atlantic Ocean.

When the ship docked in Nova Scotia, they were met by more Red Cross workers and put on a troop train to Chicago, where they changed for New York. There they were put in a taxi by another Red Cross worker and the driver brought them to the children's grandparents' house on Park Avenue. Maureen was given $50 and was thanked. But nobody even asked her if she had anywhere to go or if she knew anyone in New York. Fortunately in those days $50 was a lot of money and she was able to pay for a hotel room for a few days. In her rush, she had left her savings behind at Annie's place in London. But she was very competent and bright, and soon she got a job in a doctor's surgery.

8
—

THE MOVE TO KILDARE

My sisters Paddy, Joan and Dolores were working for families in Dublin, and Maureen was now in America. That left Timmy and me with my father. One night he told me he was going to put me in a convent in Naas and he was keeping Timmy with him. He wanted to turn him into a jockey. I was devastated at the thought of leaving Timmy. I cried and cried but to no avail. My father said that he would give me two shillings and sixpence and I could come home to visit. That did not make me feel any better. Timmy begged him to let me stay but there was no changing my father's decision. Timmy cried hard. When I was leaving for the convent, wearing an old green wool coat with one side longer than the other, Timmy was standing on the pathway to our house chewing on his jacket and crying his heart out. My father told me to hop on the back of his bike and off we went. It was a long and very uncomfortable trip over the bumpy roads to Naas.

The black iron gates swung back to a path leading to the door of the Convent of Mercy in Naas. It was a massive structure. Daddy slipped me the two and sixpence he had promised me for going there. I stuck it in my coat pocket. We rang the bell and the door was immediately opened by a cheerful, fat nun, who ushered us into a waiting room warmed by a fire. A very cold-demeanoured mother superior entered the room and shook my father's hand. She nodded to me and sat down.

My father told her that my mother was dead and he could not take care of me himself. At first she said that at eleven years of age I was too young but Daddy told her that I was very self-sufficient and that I loved to sing. That's when he sowed the seeds of disaster for me! With that she took me out to a hall where there was a piano and asked me what I would like to sing. I said 'When I Grow Too Old To Dream'. She accompanied me while I sang but I was so scared and upset that I could not finish. She told me to go back to the waiting room.

After a short while she came in alone. I never got a chance to say goodbye to my father. She told me to follow her upstairs to a long dormitory and pointed to a cot by a window where she said I was to sleep. It was getting late and we would be having tea. The girls had tea in the kitchen. She took me there, where girls older than me were setting the table for tea. I was introduced as the new girl and told that as of tomorrow my job would be to set the table for tea before prayers in the chapel, which was in the grounds. After tea I helped wash dishes that came from the nuns' dining room. Then we went to bed. I lay awake thinking of Timmy and what he would be doing. I cried myself to sleep. I was lonely and very homesick.

Next morning, I awoke to a nun's voice telling us to

get ready for prayers. At the bottom of my bed was a big navy-blue jumper and long navy gymslip with a white shirt. Still, a uniform was better than what I was used to. I looked out. It was a cold morning; the ivy around the window glistened with raindrops. They looked like tiny diamonds. I thought to myself that Daddy had left without saying a word to me. I felt very rejected. I was slightly surprised to discover that although I was in a convent school, I would not be going to any classes. My job would be ironing the nuns' gimps and setting the table. The gimps were damp and heavily starched. The iron was heated in a coal fire and then wiped clean. If you got any creases in the gimps while ironing them it was very hard to get them out. It took a long time but in the end I became very good at the job.

One day while I was setting the table in the kitchen a group of nuns were complaining about how dirty the statue of St Patrick was. The statue was in the garden and one of them came in and asked me to wash it that afternoon. I was given a bucket of soapy water and some rags. I could barely reach his head. I didn't like the job very much. I wondered why the birds would shit all over the patron saint, and they were still at it while I was cleaning it. I decided I would never want to be a patron saint if that was the thanks you got!

One day I naively told one of the girls that I had money and she went off and sneaked on me to one of the nuns. Soon after I was told that if I had money I had to turn it in and it would be returned to me when I left. I said nothing. I made no friends because the others were all older than me and I felt intimidated by them. I missed out on the chats. I never really got into the swing of things. You know, it's funny but I don't remember any of the girls there. From the kitchen window, I remember, I could see day-girls playing in the schoolyard below and I felt so excluded.

One day, Mother Superior was expecting a bishop from Dublin for afternoon tea. She asked me to sing, saying that the bishop would enjoy it. I asked her if I could go home for a visit soon but she said I could not leave the grounds. I almost burst into tears. When the bishop finished tea I was called to the piano. I started to sing a song my father learned in America and had taught me:

There was a jolly nigger and his name was Uncle
Ned;
He died not so very long ago.
He had no hair on the top of his head,
The place where the hair ought to grow.

Hang up your fiddle and your bow,
Lay down your shovel and your hoe,
For there's no more work for poor Uncle Ned:
He's gone where the good niggers go.

One frosty morning the good nigger died;
The darkies cried like rain,
For they knew very well when they put him in his
grave
That they'd never see his baldy head again.
For there's no more work for poor Uncle Ned
He's gone where the good niggers go.

There was complete silence and very coldly the mother superior said, 'Go up to your room.' I felt that they were upset with me but I didn't know why. I climbed the stairs and waited. I sat on my bed and looked out the window. I could see the bishop leaving and saying goodbye to the nuns. They opened the gates to let his car out and waved as he left. Mother Superior came to the dorm and looked at me with such disgust. 'Why did you sing that song?' she asked. I told her that my father had taught it to me and I did not know that it was bad. She shook her finger in my face and said, 'Don't you ever sing that song again!' I promised that I wouldn't. Then she said, 'What a waste of a beautiful voice to sing a song like that.' I again promised her that I would never sing it again. She said that she would speak to my father about it.

I don't know how I remembered all those words. I don't know where that song came from. My father had taught it to me and he called it an Irish song! I didn't think of 'nigger' as a bad word – I didn't even understand it. We didn't think the word 'gollywog' was a bad word then either. The nun left, and before stomping down the stairs, called back, 'Don't forget to set the table in the kitchen, then prayers, extra prayers.' I went downstairs and set the table and hung my coat on a rack by the back door. We went to the chapel for prayers. My penance was ten Hail Marys extra. Then we went back for tea. I offered to do all the dishes as well.

I was alone now. When I was finished doing all the dishes I set the table for breakfast. I looked out the kitchen window and saw that it was suddenly snowing quite heavily. I looked around to make sure no one was around, grabbed my coat and quickly ran outside. I ran across the garden towards the back of the chapel. I could hear a voice calling me from an upper window. It was the mother superior. I ignored her and ran through the back of the chapel. There was some kind of service going on but I continued on and ran down the aisle and out the front door. Luckily for me, there was now a blizzard outside. I felt the two and sixpence in my pocket. I hurried to the bus stop with my head down to keep the snow out of my face. I ducked into the nearest doorway for shelter the building turned out to be a pub. I looked up and thought I had been caught. But it was only a reflection of myself in a mirror.

As I started to hurry on again, the bus came to a halt at the pub. I jumped on and told the driver that I was going to Brownstown. He said that would be sixpence. I gave him my half-crown and he handed me two shillings change. We set off into the darkness and it was late in the evening when we arrived in Brownstown. I was over-joyed to see my old town and started down the road I knew so well. My breath was steamy in the cold and it was still snowing. I shoved my hands into my coat pockets. I could hear the soft crunch of the snow under my feet. Soon I was at the door of our house and my heart was pounding. I was scared. I didn't know what my father would do to me. I was also surprised to find the house in darkness. I opened the door and the reflection of the snow illuminated the inside of the house. To my astonish-ment the house was bare. I went from room to room in panic but there was no furniture. The place was empty; everyone was gone. There was only an discarded old pillow on the floor. Tears welled up in my eyes but I was too tired to cry. I took the pillow and, knowing there was nothing else to do, propped myself up in a corner of the kitchen and finally fell asleep from exhaustion with my head falling forward every now and again.

Suddenly a noise jolted me awake and I looked out towards the window. There in the moonlight, staring in the window at me, was a huge, hairy head with two great black orbs rolling back and forth in seas of white. For a minute I thought it was a banshee. Then I saw a mouth open and close with spittle dropping from it. Then it started to moo. I almost cried with relief. I wondered what had become of Daisy but guessed my father had discarded her too.

I fell back asleep and soon it was morning. I was cold, stiff and hungry. I pulled my coat around me for more warmth. It was bright and clear outside; the birds were singing and I tried to think what to do. I decided to enquire in the village as to the whereabouts of my father and Timmy. I was told to take a bus to Kildare town, where they had heard that Daddy had got work on a stud farm. The bus came and it was empty. I told the driver that I was going to Kildare town. The fare was threepence. I sat at a window seat. The bus driver was smoking a Woodbine and the aroma made me remember the time Timmy and I stole one of my father's cigarettes and smoked it by the side of the house. We both got deathly ill. Everybody was being really nice to us because they thought we were really sick. We never dared to tell anyone what we had done.

When the bus driver called 'Kildare town', I hopped off

and immediately found a little shop that had hot cross buns. I bought two at a penny each and couldn't gobble them down fast enough. Then I started making enquiries about the whereabouts of my father. I was sure it was not the National Stud, which was the largest and most important stud farm in the world and belonged to the government of Ireland. Eventually, I was directed to Hartigan's, a place I had heard my father mention. I found it just outside the town. As I went into the stables I saw a young boy dressed in jodhpurs. I thought for a minute it was Timmy. It wasn't but the boy said he would lead me to him and he told me my father was riding a horse in the paddock. Imagine my relief.

Timmy was mucking out one of the stables. When he saw me he dropped the rake and flung his arms around me. When my father came back and saw me he was absolutely livid. And do you know what he was mad about? That I could have done that to the nuns – not whether I had been unhappy or not. He said that I would be going straight back to the convent. Timmy begged him to let me stay. But my father said no: I had to go back and face what I had done.

He said that he would have to stay there and work but Timmy would show me where they were staying and he would talk to me when he got home. Timmy and I skipped off down the road, happy for at least the present. Timmy told me how pleased he was that I was there and I told him how sad I had been in the convent and how I had got into trouble for singing 'The Jolly Nigger'. I told him that he should never sing that song again.

My father and Timmy were staying at a house nearby,

run by an older woman. She was single. The house had only two bedrooms and the woman rented one of them out to Daddy and Timmy. There was only one bed in the room so they had to share a bed. When Timmy and I got to the house he made me some tea and gave me a slice of soda bread with country butter and sugar on top of it.

Soon my father arrived back. He dropped his bike on the ground outside, rushed in and slapped me hard across the face. I didn't really expect him to hug and reassure me. My nose started bleeding. Timmy cried and told him to stop. 'She's going back,' my father said. I told him I would run away again if he sent me back and the next time I wouldn't come back to him.

I stayed there that night. We all slept in the one bed, with Timmy in the middle. I don't know if we got any sleep. Mind you, beds had always been scarce and as children we had got used to sleeping together. I lay looking up at the one light bulb in the ceiling and thought about the first time we got electricity in Brownstown. It was such a special occasion that my father said we could all go to the movies to see *Frankenstein*. That was a real treat! I was fascinated by the light bulb hanging down from the kitchen ceiling. When everybody had gone I spent the whole evening turning the light on and off and on and off. I couldn't understand how it worked. I thought if I turned it on slowly I would see how it worked as it went on. As I lay there in the bed next to Timmy and watched the light bulb I drifted off to sleep, just happy to be back with him.

The next day, Daddy phoned the convent from the stud farm. Timmy told me that he had overheard Daddy talking to the mother superior and evidently they did not want me back. Well, after my rendition of 'The Jolly Nigger' they weren't too impressed. And I suppose I had also got the better of them by escaping.

I started to earn a few bob cleaning out fireplaces, washing windows and working in the kitchen at the Hartigan's stud farm when they had dinner parties. I was allowed to push the food out through the serving window of the kitchen but not permitted to be in the dining room because I was too young. I suppose Mrs Hartigan was afraid of being accused of exploiting me. She was a very cold and formidable woman and she scared me.

Our father turned against the woman of the house. He didn't seem to have too high a regard for women. We moved to a house down the street which had a room with two separate beds. One was for me and the other was for Timmy and Dad. The house was owned by a couple. The man of the house worked at the coalyard and his clothes, hands and face were always black. The woman had lost a baby shortly after it was born. As soon as her husband had gone to work, she would start to lay out her dead baby's clothes. The husband told me if I saw the 'missus' crying over the baby clothes, I was to tell him, but I never did – I think she was afraid of him.

Timmy and I lived in this house for the next few years. My father was off on his own a lot – we rarely saw him. We were not allowed access to the rest of the house unless we were cleaning, sweeping or gardening. My father was supposedly paying rent for the room but I suspect he had traded our housekeeping services against room and board.

The people of the house used me for serving meals at their table and doing household chores. Food was very scarce for Timmy and me. We didn't know any of our neighbours except by name. They didn't want to know us and made that very plain. We had no clothes to speak of, except whatever was on our backs; these clothes had been bought at the tinker's market. I longed for a nice dress and used to cut out the ads of pretty dresses from the newspapers and save them to look at. Timmy spent a lot of his time chasing after an old bicycle wheel with a stick – he would run all over Kildare town with it.

The man of the house told us one evening that he'd bought a plot on the turf bog and that Timmy and I were going turf-cutting with him. He said I could ride the missus's bike, with Timmy on the back. We used to catch the sods as he threw them up with the *sleán* and spread them out on the ground to dry. When he was finished the whole plot we had to go back on our own each day and 'foot' the turf (stand three sods upright, with a fourth sod on top) to dry it in the sun and wind. We had very little to eat on those long days but we would make a little fire with pieces of dry turf and boil water in an old can for tea. That tea tasted really good.

One day a man working on the plot next to us asked me did I want to earn sixpence. When I said I did, he told me to take it out of his trouser pocket. When I reached in there was no pocket there, just bare skin, and he clapped his hand over mine, holding it there. I yelled to him to stop and tried to pull my hand away. When Timmy saw what was going on he picked up the bogman's *sleán* and, holding it up to the man's face, calmly told him to let me go. 'You're a cheeky little lad, aren't you!' laughed the man, pushing me over. Timmy said to me afterwards that he would have punched him but I started crying and said I was all right.

When the turf was dry our landlord brought along a little donkey and cart he had borrowed and told us to go and get the turf. We did that and brought it back to the house and stacked it up in the back. A few days later he was outside selling the turf to his neighbours – we got nothing at all in return for all our hard work.

Timmy and I loved to go walking and exploring. When we heard that the famous tenor John McCormack lived in the nearby town of Monasterevin, we took it into our heads to walk there. We stopped at a little sweetshop and asked which was his house. The owner pointed to a house on the road to Athy, surrounded by a big wall. It turned out that the wall was studded with pieces of broken glass so that nobody could climb over, so we sat down on a grassy patch next to it. Timmy had a voice like an angel. He knew nearly all McCormack's songs, and as we sat he began to sing his favourite which was 'Little Boy Blue' by Eugene Field (1850-95):

The little toy dog was covered with dust,
   But sturdy and staunch he stands;
And the little toy soldier is red with rust,
   And his musket moulds in his hands.
Time was when the little toy dog was new,
   And the soldier was passing fair;
And that was the time when our Little Boy Blue
   Kissed them and put them there.

'Now don't you go till I come,' he said,
'And don't you make any noise!'
So toddling off to his trundle bed
He dreamt of his pretty toys;
And, as he was dreaming, an angel song
Awakened our Little Boy Blue.
Oh! the years are many, the years are long,
But the little toy friends are true!

Suddenly the big iron gate opened and a man wearing a long black coat and cap came out. He came over to us and asked what we were doing. Timmy told him how much we loved John McCormack and that we knew all his songs. The man said Mr McCormack was not there and that he was the caretaker, but when 'the Master' returned from Italy he would tell him he had some faithful admirers. We were so pleased and happy that he was going to pass on the message that it made up for not seeing him in person. Soon after that we heard the sad news that John McCormack had died. We were both heartbroken and Timmy was very upset when he told me.

Then I got a terrible blow. Just before my twelfth birthday, my father, through the church, got me a job as a nanny in Dublin with the Taylor family. My father expected me to follow in the footsteps of Dolores, Joan and Paddy, whom he had also fixed up in houses in Dublin.

The Taylors had a little boy aged about two and Mrs Taylor was expecting her second baby. I found it strange to be part of a loving, normal household but I also found it very lonely. I missed Timmy enormously. One day while I was there my first period began. I thought I was dying. But Mrs Taylor explained to me that it was a natural thing and she gave me some connections with feelings and caring. She mothered me in some ways.

While I was there I had my twelfth birthday. I didn't realise that it was my birthday that particular day. I was so surprised when Otto Bruch showed up at the Taylors' door with a big cream birthday cake for me. I was not allowed to see him and he was sent away.

I do not think the Taylors were happy about Otto coming to their house because the next thing I knew I was on a bus back to Kildare. I was so afraid to face my father,

Sheila and Otto in O'Connell St Dublin

I stopped and went to a movie on the way back. When I saw him he was livid. He went to the military camp in Brownstown where Otto was interned and complained about him. I never saw Otto again. Then the Taylors hired my sister Joan to replace me.

I was fifteen when the war ended in 1945. The Germans were going home. One day, while Paddy was on a visit from Dublin to Brownstown, Hans Gobel took her for a walk. He told her they were sending him back to Germany but he didn't want to go back. So he picked up a huge rock, handed it to her and lay down, then begged her to smash both his knees so that he could postpone his departure from Ireland. But she couldn't do it.

The Germans left on buses and were going to be shipped home by boat. The townspeople threw rocks at the buses because they had learned the news about the concentration camps from newsreels. Otto had given me a pin when I had first met him. I thought it was pretty and I used to wear it on my dress. We were all innocently wearing them. One day, an Irish soldier noticed my pin on me and asked, 'Why are you wearing that swastika?' I didn't know what he meant. He said to me, 'If I were you I would get rid of that or you will have rocks thrown at you and be called a Nazi.' I wondered what would happen to poor Otto.

While we were living in Kildare town I saw a poster about a dance being held at the military camp, with free admission. I wore a short sweater and an A-line wool skirt. I remember wearing my long hair loose but pinned back from my face with a side-grip. Daddy was away at the time so I could not ask his permission. I had such a great time that I didn't realise how late it was. Erin Doyle, a girl I had met at the dance, said she lived in Kildare and we could walk home together.

It started raining on the way home and we got soaked. She told me I could sleep at her house since it was nearer. They didn't have an extra bed but there was an armchair in front of a fading turf fire and she said that I could sleep there. It was nice and warm. The next day I returned home and Daddy was back. He was livid and refused to believe me when I told him what had happened. So he dragged me back to the house to show him where I had slept. Mrs Doyle was there and she told him I was telling him the truth. He threatened to kill me if I ever did that again. I never did.

9
—

THE VOYAGE TO THE NEW WORLD

Just before my sixteenth birthday, in 1946, my sister Maureen came back to Ireland with the news that we were all going to America. Everyone thought she was a movie star because she looked so glamorous and beautiful. Suddenly everyone wanted to know us and we were so proud. At that time, after the war, they wanted young people to work in America.

My father was in England and Maureen went to the American Embassy in Dublin to apply for our American passports. She told them we were American citizens but they said they needed my father's consent. So she tracked him down in England and he had to come back. He was furious, shouting, 'Do you know the trouble you caused me?' But we didn't care, we were so excited. Our only concern was that he might refuse to give his consent out of sheer spite.

To acquire American passports we had to renounce our Irish citizenship. (I have since acquired an Irish passport.) Maureen, Timmy and I took a bus to Dublin to see Joan, Dolores and Paddy, who were working there as house-maids. We met at Bewley's Café in Grafton Street and there we had the best meal we had ever had in our lives – it was made more special by the fact that we were all there together.

When everything was taken care of and we had obtained our passports to America, it was arranged for us to board the *Gripsholm*, which had been a hospital ship during the war, but which was now a Swedish-American liner taking emigrants to America. It was making a stop at Cobh Harbour, Cork, on 14 March 1946 and we were to take a train from Dublin the day before. The day we were leaving Kildare to take the bus to Dublin I said brief goodbyes to Noeleen, the girl whose shoes I used to help break in, and some other girls I knew. The previous day, Timmy and I had gone to the graveyards and put cowslips on Mama's grave and snowdrops on Victor's. We felt unbearably sad as we prayed over them.

We took the steam train from Dublin to Cork and changed for Cobh. The train ride to Cork was very exciting. None of us except Maureen and Daddy had ever been on a train before. It seemed the journey was over much too fast and all of a sudden we were going to the dock, where the *Gripsholm* was anchored out in the bay. They were embarking people on the link boats known as tenders. There were hundreds of people leaving and I wondered if half of Ireland was going to America.

While we were waiting, Timmy and I decided to take a walk around town, not realising that everyone was waiting for us to board the very last tender going out to our ship. We were oblivious to the time and were very surprised when a policeman came up to us and asked if we were the Connolly youngsters. We nodded, looking scared.

When he told us they were all waiting for us back at the quayside we dashed back, barely in time to board the tender – but in time to get a good slap on the back of the head from my father, who was furious. We were crammed together like sardines, but as the tender pulled slowly away from the dock, a crowd of people standing on the quays – priests, nuns and loved ones who had tearfully said goodbye to relatives – began singing in chorus, 'Come Back to Erin'. I was so overcome with emotion that I sobbed uncontrollably as the crowd slowly became dimmer and dimmer in the distance. The day we sailed out of Ireland was my sixteenth birthday.

I think I must have been sick for almost half the ten-day trip. The first five days I spent lying in my bunk, unable to help myself. Finally, a young sailor came down and carried me up on deck, put me in a deckchair and brought me some liquids to drink. I was soon back on my feet, but recovery brought another hardship to face: we were all lined up for the vaccinations which were obligatory for entry into the US. When my turn came to be given my shot I didn't move forward immediately, so the doctor gave me a rough push, which almost knocked me over, much to my dismay.

My sister still has our dining-room table card. My sisters Paddy, Joan and Dolores were now very attractive girls and they had a wonderful time on board because the sailors were very taken with them. When my father came on deck looking for them, I would sound a warning signal so that they would keep hidden in the lifeboats. The crew would meet them after their shifts. Pretty soon the captain complained to my father that he could not find his sailors, so that put an end to all their fun. As you can imagine, my father was seriously unimpressed.

During the voyage my father discovered that my sister Paddy had kept a lot of Nazi souvenirs from the German prisoners she had met. He found them when he went through her stuff. He had a fit and tipped them over the side of the boat before we arrived in America. Lucky for us he did or we might have found ourselves being sent home on the next boat.

All in all, I had much less fun than they did, because as well as being seasick, I found the experience of being in the middle of a great ocean very frightening, and not seeing any land for such a long time was disorientating. The big whales which often came near the ship worried me so much that I was afraid to sleep but I didn't tell anyone about this, not even Timmy, who was having a great time. He was just having fun and, being a boy, spent most of the voyage exploring the boat with other kids. It was the first time I felt that Timmy and I were drifting apart. I felt very much alone and apprehensive about the new life that lay ahead of us.

On 24 March 1946, the tenth day after leaving Ireland, we passed the Statue of Liberty. There was great excitement; everyone was up on deck. When we finally docked at New York, my first impression on looking from the rail was of lots of yellow cars lined up on the dock. I blurted out, 'Daddy, everyone in America has a yellow car!' This was before I realised that the men standing by the yellow cars were calling out 'Taxi! Taxi!' My second impression was of food! I could see members of the Red Cross giving out coffee and doughnuts for everyone in Arrivals.

When we disembarked from the *Gripsholm* my father was almost refused entry by immigration officials because he had severe varicose veins in both his legs and they thought he would be unemployable. But we were American citizens and able to sponsor him and he knew some racehorse owners who would give him a job working the horses. So he got through, much to his relief.

We assembled all our belongings, which consisted mainly of my father's trunk, his overfull Navy sacks and our tattered, shabby suitcases. My father hailed one of those 'yellow cars' and told the driver to take us to the nearest subway station to go to Brooklyn. The taxi driver

Paddy, Sheila (top), Daddy, Timmy, New York, 1946

was very friendly; he wanted to know if we came from Ireland and he welcomed us to America. Suddenly on the way to the subway when the driver put his hand out to turn left a police car bumped him accidentally. Luckily there was no damage and when the policeman came up to the window the driver asked him had he not seen his hand signal. The policeman said, 'No', so my father piped up, 'And if he stuck his leg out you wouldn't have seen that either.' The cab driver said apologetically, 'I've just picked them up from the dock off the Irish boat.'

'Oh!' the policeman said to my father. 'Well, you'd better watch your tongue here, Paddy!' My sister Paddy thought he was talking to her so she answered, 'Yes, sir!' My father laughed all the way to the station.

At the subway station my father gave us all tokens to put into the turnstile. Paddy went first and when the turnstile went down she held on to it because she thought she had broken it. In the meantime people were lined up behind us waiting and yelling, 'Go ahead, go ahead!' and they were looking at us as if we came from Mars. Paddy finally let go. While we were waiting for the train we were in everyone's way with all our stuff, and a porter accidentally ran over Dolores's foot with a big, heavy trolley cart. She screamed with pain and was limping afterwards but he paid no attention and kept on going. We had to calm her down.

When the train came we all piled on with our stuff. My father knew which stop we were to get off at for Coney Island; my sister Maureen had arranged for us to stay with a Mrs Gallagher, an old friend of my parents, who lived alone and was elderly. When we arrived at our destination we all got off, but my sister Paddy had left something behind on the train. She ran back in to get it but the doors closed before she could make it, and the train took off. We all stood there watching her alarmed face through the window as she zipped past us.

We waited at the station because someone told us they were sure she would be put back on the next train on the other side of the platform – and they were right. Soon a smiling Paddy arrived on the next train, very relieved to be back with us.

My father said it was not far to Mrs Gallagher's house, that it was within walking distance from the station. We must have looked like a right bunch of down-and-outs, dragging our baggage along the streets. To make matters worse, my father said he knew a short cut, which turned out to be across a busy highway. It was raining by now and he told us each to carry something and run fast across the highway when there was a break in the traffic. We made it across, dodging cars that were blowing their horns at us, and waited at the other side for Timmy and Daddy to carry the trunk across. Finally there was another break in the whizzing traffic and they made a dash for it, hauling the trunk between them. We watched in horror as a big truck hurtled towards them in the pouring rain. They dropped the trunk and ran for it, while the truck swerved and the driver honked his horn and shook his fist. Undeterred, they darted back to rescue the precious trunk and rejoin us, the sound of honking still following them.

It was night time when we finally reached Mrs Gallagher's little house. She lived in Bay Fifty-third Street on a dirt road near the beach. We were exhausted but she couldn't have been more kind, plying us with potato salad, cold meats and coleslaw. We had never had that kind of food before and it was very good. The house was very crowded with all of us in it and there were only a few beds, so we bunked together once again. I have to say I was delighted to be on dry land.

We had been in America only about a week when I became very homesick for Ireland. I found America too different and cried all the time, begging my father to send me back. When Timmy asked me why I wanted to go back, I said I missed the green of the countryside and felt surrounded by concrete. Timmy said *he* didn't miss fetching buckets of water from the pumps down the road and not having enough to eat, but this only reinforced my feeling of distance from him and my loneliness. One of the main reasons for Irish people wanting to go back home when they got to the States was the lack of singing. I guess I just missed the whole way of life I had left behind and felt uncomfortable in my new surroundings.

10

NEW YORK, NEW YORK

After a while we all began to settle in to a new way of life. My sister Dolores fell in love with a boy on our street. His name was Charlie Davis and he worked in the telephone company. The company needed staff, so Dolores and Joan went for an interview and got jobs as telephone operators. Paddy was employed as a store detective and Maureen, who had met a marine sergeant on the voyage across, was now married and living in an apartment in uptown New York, where she was working for a doctor. My father took Timmy with him to the stables, where they had a room. Before he left, he enrolled me in a local high school, which I guess was convenient and in theory seemed like a good idea.

I was completely lost at the school and stood out from all the other kids. I couldn't make friends because they called me 'square' and referred to me as the 'Polish' girl. I didn't understand that and kept insisting that I was Irish but they just laughed. Then one day another girl and I were sent home because we had lice in our hair. We were given lotion to put on our heads and told not to come back until it was cleared up. I felt so humiliated and ashamed.

One day during my enforced quarantine period, I saw a sign that said 'Help Wanted' in the window of Woolworth's Five and Dime store; so I applied and got the job. I had made up my mind that I was never going back to school. The work was only part-time but it was my first job and I was deliriously happy to be making money of my own. When I got my first pay cheque, the first thing I bought was the promised pretty yellow dress for myself.

Little by little, I stopped being homesick; things were helped by Maureen's frequent visits to us in Brooklyn, to which I always looked forward. She wanted me to come into the doctor's office where she worked for a check-up – something I had never had – so I went. She told me to remove my upper clothing and I was so shocked: 'You mean I have to take off my bra!' She was amazed that I had never been to a doctor before. I was allowed to keep my bra on after she told the doctor how upset I was. He was very kind and told me I was in good health.

Dolores and Charlie announced their engagement and forthcoming wedding in June in the local Catholic church. We were all going to be her bridesmaids, and Maureen, who was expecting her first baby at the time, was to be matron of honour.

Mrs Gallagher's house was too small for us and also a bit unsafe – almost any time you turned on a switch you would get an electric shock. Fortunately, the mother of Dolores's fiancé offered to rent us the basement part of her house, which was nice and roomy; so we moved over there.

After a while, as my confidence grew in my first job, I

decided I wanted to earn more money. I called the telephone company where Dolores and her fiancé were working and asked for an interview. I got an appointment almost at once. The woman who interviewed me was very warm and friendly and told me I could have a job but that I could not work as a speaking operator because of my Irish accent. She said people might not understand me. Until I came to America I had never realised that different countries had different accents – I thought I had no accent at all! So I was put on a board called a tandem, which meant connecting the operator to outlying local cities. I became quite good and quick at the job. It became something of a challenge to me to memorise the whole board. That was how I got around my problem with numbers. I couldn't believe how much money I was earning. Everyone was so nice to me there and I made lots of friends. I had never felt so content before. I thrived with their encouragement after all the years of being put down by my father and the nuns.

Sometimes I worked a double shift from nine am to one pm, then six to ten pm, so I had most of the afternoon free. Going home late at night I would sometimes fall asleep on the train. One night I slept past my stop and got off at the next one. Because it was raining, I decided to take a short cut home through a deserted street. I thought if I walked quickly through it, I would be OK. I had my umbrella open so my line of vision was restricted. As I hurried along I sensed someone behind me. I turned around to see a man following me. Frightened, I tried to run away but I stumbled and fell, and he grabbed me and took my umbrella from me. He began to hit me with it. I was kicking and screaming as I struggled with him.

Suddenly in the distance, a voice called out and with that he took fright and he ran away. Soon people in pyjamas came running out towards me. The man who had called out was expecting his wife home when he heard me screaming and thought I was her. That is what saved me. The police came to drive me home and by the time I got inside the house, I was hysterical, bruised and shaken.

The next morning, the police came back with a big book of photos of criminals but I could not identify anyone because it had been too dark and rainy. Only a short time after that I was coming home late on the train after work when I found I was the only passenger in the carriage. A man got on at one of the stops and just kept staring at me. Suddenly he came towards me and stood there exposing himself. I was terrified and I screamed. At the next stop he ran out. From then on I was very careful and only got into a car that had several people in it. On later shifts when the weather was bad, I decided to stay over in the telephone company's dormitory.

Dolores and Charlie married and got their own apartment. That left just Paddy, Joan and me. Because of the incidents on my way home, we decided to move again and found a place in a safer area near the subway so we didn't have far to walk. It was the first floor of an elderly Italian couple's home on McDonald Avenue on Coney Island. They had no children and loved to cook so there was always an aroma of pasta and Italian sausage coming up the stairs. They always wanted us to eat: '*Mange, mange*,' they would say. Finally we started to sneak into our room because we got so tired of having to sit at their table and be force-fed. They were very nice but their kindness was too demanding on our time and privacy.

Paddy was a store detective. Once I asked her, 'What would you do if I came in and took something? Would you turn me in?'

'Of course I would!' she replied proudly. So one day I decided to call her bluff. I brazenly went into the store and nicked a purse, thinking that she'd see me. I walked out of the store. Nothing happened! Then I realised I couldn't go back in. What was I going to do! I finally decided to go to a church and put something in the poor box as conscience money. I hadn't the nerve to tell Paddy about this until recently and she couldn't believe it, because she thought she caught everyone that ever took anything from that store. 'Can you imagine what my manager would have done had she caught you?' she said.

I always wanted a fun-fur coat but I couldn't pay for one in full and I was under-age for signing for goods on credit. I think the price was $100. So Joan, who was two years older than me, said, 'Let's pretend you are Dolores.' But we kept calling each other by the wrong names in front of the manager. He said to Joan, 'Well, if her name is Dolores, why are you calling her Sheila?'

'Oh, it's just a nickname we use,' we said. By the time we got outside we were practically hysterical with laughter. And do you know, when I got that fur coat home I hated it! So I went back in the next day and said, 'You're going to have to take it back because I'm under-age and I signed that thing and I don't have a job and I can't pay for it.' Oh, he was furious and said he wasn't going to take it back. In the end I just took the coat off and left it there and walked out. Luckily, they never billed me for it.

One day I saw that a swimsuit contest was going to be held at the beach on Coney Island. Encouraged by Maureen, I bought a black velour one-piece suit and entered the contest. The singer Vic Damone was the judge and he picked out both Paddy and me as winners. Vic and I became casual acquaintances. There was no prize, just a photo in the paper, but it was fun. Then at the telephone company, they had a contest called 'The Office Orchid' to find the most popular girl in the building. I was selected and won lots of prizes.

District Six "Office Orchid"

Local No. 1's contribution to the Journal American's recent "Office Orchid" contest was a pretty colleen from County Kildare, Eire, known as Sheila Connolly.

Maureen had signed up with a modelling agency and recommended I do likewise. She assured me that I was very pretty and said I could be a model like her. I had never thought of myself in that way before. She encouraged me to get some photos taken and said she would take me to some agencies. It gave me a whole new perspective on things.

One night when I was at Maureen's apartment my father was there, and when I told him about my plan to try to become a model he picked up a flashlight, turned it on my face and said, 'This is the only spotlight you'll ever get; a maid is the only thing you'll ever become – you're nothing!' I was incensed and burst out, 'You killed our mother with heartbreak!' whereupon he put his fist up to my nose and exclaimed, 'You know you almost died when you were ten months old and I'm sorry you didn't!' He was referring to the double pneumonia I had as a baby, when the doctor told my parents to make arrangements for my burial. But I was a fighter and took a turn for the better overnight and survived.

That was to be one of the last conversations that I had with my father for many years. I don't think he was aware of the lasting impact this had on me. I don't think he cared. It wouldn't even have occurred to him to apologise. He was often brutal. The strange thing is that my sisters Joan and Maureen, whom he treated the worst, ended up taking care of him.

Anyone who ever met my father, in a bar or wherever, loved him. They thought he was the funniest man ever. If he was thirsty he had to go and have a beer. Even if he was in heavy traffic, in New York, say, he would just abandon his car wherever he pleased. It didn't matter if there was no parking space. Of course the police would come into the bar to get him and he would say to them, 'Well, if you can get that car started, you go ahead.' And they would believe him. He was such a chancer!

I started thinking about getting a portfolio of photographic shots together. I found out about a school of photography where they used you as a model to experiment with the camera and then gave you free photos, although most were unusable. One of the photographers told me one day that I was a nice kid and that he would hate to see me get hurt, because he felt I would never be a model. That annoyed me so much that, from that day on, I was perversely determined to become a model. I felt I learned a lot from his remark and it gave me a little more strength to go ahead and be prepared for the hard knocks of life. Perhaps in some ways, my father inadvertently helped me too. He certainly toughened me up!

I bought all the young fashion magazines, like *Seventeen, American Girl, Harper's Bazaar,* and studied the models' clothes, hairstyles and poses. I cut my hair short, which suited the shape of my face much better, and bought some smart, classic clothes. Maureen took me to one agency but she didn't like the way they were trying to persuade me to pose in lingerie.

It was very hard work, walking all over New York to the different agencies, leaving composite photos, hoping they would look at them and call me for a job. Then back to the telephone company in the evening to work. I really liked my job there but the idea of being a junior fashion model was naturally more exciting. One day I saw from an ad in a magazine that the Hartford Agency was looking for new models, so I phoned for an appointment. I got an interview with a Mr Deering, who told me I had to have a portfolio of photos and sent me to a photographer whom he knew who was good and not expensive. Then he said we would see.

Hartford's offices on Forty-eighth Street and Madison Avenue were very plush. Mr Hartford was very wealthy. He owned a chain of supermarkets and also spent a lot of time at the agency – his office was right by the elevator so that he could see all the girls coming into his place. He always waved and gave a big smile. I had my photo-sitting, which went very well – the photographer helped me to make up, telling me to use lots of mascara and pancake. I really liked the way it looked because it made me seem so glamorous. I returned to Mr Deering's office and was told that the photos were OK and that he would give me a chance. I didn't tell him that I was still working at the telephone company and was on a free shift. Since I had nearly all day free I didn't think it was necessary. I suppose I was also afraid he would look down on such an occupation.

My first modelling job was with Sears Patterns Catalogue as a regular, which meant I had to be available when they called me. At the start this was only several times a month. The pay was $250 per month and the contract was non-exclusive, so I could also accept other jobs in the meantime. I was next offered some work by *Seventeen* magazine. After a while offers of work were so frequent that I thought I would quit my job at the telephone company. When I did hand in my notice, they were very sorry to hear I was leaving. We parted on good terms and they told me that if I ever wanted to come back I would always be welcome and would be offered the same degree of seniority.

I decided I wanted to live on my own nearer New York City so that I wouldn't have to travel so far. I started looking for a place to live and soon saw an ad for a private room in a nice apartment in the Upper East Side. It was to be let by a mother and daughter, who were both teachers. They said I could have the room for $45 a month. The restrictions were no visitors or kitchen privileges, but since I didn't cook, that was fine.

One day I was sitting in the booking office of the agency when I overheard a call coming in from Ponds for girls, with blonde hair only, for a full-page colour ad. I heard the address and decided to go anyway and leave a photo with the well-known movie-star photographer George Hurrell. I was greeted upon arrival by his wife. She asked me if I was Irish (because of my accent), then took me back into the studio and introduced me to her husband, who took some test shots of me right there and then. I thanked them and returned to the agency.

Upon my return, I was conscious that everyone at the agency was looking at me coldly. Finally they told me that I was booked for the 'Angel Face' ad. They were furious with me and warned me that if I ever went on a call that I hadn't been allocated again they would dismiss me from the agency. But I was in seventh heaven and didn't care what they said to me. After the Ponds Angel Face ad came out in all the fashion magazines, I was booked for the Sweetheart soap ad, where they use a name to endorse

the product: 'Sheila Connolly uses Sweetheart soap.' They gave me crates of it. I couldn't believe I was seeing my own name in print in a magazine and on my own soap! If I had died right then I would have been happy.

The other models at the agency were very friendly and often invited me to their parents' homes. That is when I would feel lost, seeing parents and children together in a real home. I started doing commercials for TV, which was fun. After a few commercials, I started getting letters at the agency saying how much I resembled Elizabeth Taylor and how much alike we photographed. This similarity had its drawbacks, as I was about to discover!

At the time I was also getting interested in acting and saw in *Variety* that a picture about reform-school girls was being filmed in Central Park. They were going to need a lot of young girls in it. I looked up the name of the producer and called the studio. The casting director was a man named Kermit Love, who later designed Kermit the Frog of *The Muppet Show* fame. He told me I could come in and see him and after my interview with him he went to the producer and told him, 'I have just met an angel and she's got to be in the picture.' The producer, who was Harry Lee Danziger, said that it was all already cast, so Kermit stamped his foot and insisted, 'She's got to be in the picture.' Since there were no free parts at this stage, they decided that the movie should open with a shot of me sitting under a tree reading a book. I was to be an extra. The movie, released in 1950, was called *So Young So Bad*, with Paul Henreid of *Casablanca* fame, Rita Moreno and Anne Jackson.

11

WHEN HARRY MET SHEILA

When the movie was finished shooting I brazenly phoned the producer's office as though I were someone important and asked when I could see the rushes. I was so naive that when the secretary said, 'Oh, is this *the* Sheila Connolly?' I innocently answered, 'Yes.' She told me to hang on a moment and a male voice came on and told me to come on over. When I arrived I realised it was the producer, Harry Lee Danziger, who asked me if I had had lunch. I said I hadn't and he invited me to the famous Sardis, the in place for the stars to dine after theatre. He started kidding me about the way I said certain words, pronouncing 'th' as 't': I would say 'tree' instead of 'three' or 'ting' instead of 'thing' – so I got out of the habit. According to Harry:

Sheila looked like a real leprechaun from another world and she was adorable and as pretty as a picture – not at all sophisticated. In fact, she was very unsophisticated and unworldly. I'd never met anyone like her. She couldn't have been sweeter.

Lieutenant Harry Lee Danziger, North African Campaign, WW II

<u>HEADQUARTERS FIRST U.S. ARMORED DIVISION</u>

GENERAL ORDERS) APO 251 c/o Post master, N.Y., N.Y.
NUMBER 46   ) 1. Awards of SILVER STAR

19 May 1943.

HARRY LEE DANZIGER, (01012871), Second Lieutenant,
Company***Regiment.

For Gallantry in action on ***1943 near***, Tunisia. The attack
of his company was being delayed by the presence of enemy anti-
tank guns. Voluntarily and upon his own initiative he ordered
his tank forward alone in an attempt to locate a route of advance. The tank was subjective to heavy enemy fire but he continued forward. He then dismounted from the tank and continued
forward on foot to locate the position of the enemy guns and to
secure some enemy prisoners. While thus engaged his tank was
hit and ordered back. Although alone and armed only with a pistol
he secured the prisoners and marched them back to his company's
position. The gallantry, aggressive leadership and devotions to
duty with complete disregard for his own welfare displayed by
Second Lieutenant Danziger reflect great credit upon himself and
the command and are deserving of the highest praise.
(Medal Number 19513).

Official: By command of Major-General HARMON:
(Signature)
W.L. SCHMIDT,
Major, A.G.D.,   MAURICE ROSE
Adjutant General   Colonel, G,S,IC.,
                                        Chief of Staff

Everybody that met her fell in love with her, everyone from Orson Welles down . . . She was right out
of a box.

It was a whole new world. Harry lived with his sister
Leonore in a very large two-storey apartment on Park
Avenue. All his family were so sweet to me. We started
seeing each other quite often. We used to meet people like
the singer Dick Haymes, the actor Eddie Albert and the
blind musician George Shearing. George was amazing:
after speaking to you he could describe exactly how you
looked. Also I remember the imposing Orson Welles
coming to dinner; he was a fascinating and funny man
who used to call me 'Irish Rose'.

When Harry went away on a business trip I felt so
lonely that my sisters Joan and Paddy told me I was in
love, and I realised that they were right. I was twenty at
the time and Harry was thirty-seven.

Six months later we decided to get married, and thinking it would be amusing to elope, we drove to Arlington,
Virginia, where we were married by a judge. He played
an old scratchy record of the 'Wedding March' and I
started to cry. The newspapers got the story and my
father spotted it. Typically he was furious and threatened
to kill Harry when we got back to New York. He was
especially annoyed that the wedding had not taken place
in a Catholic church. He couldn't even be happy for me. I
wanted to protect Harry from my father but, with his
Silver Star and Purple Heart for bravery during World War
II, Harry was not worried by these threats. My father came
to our building (Joan warned me he had a knife) but the

doorman wouldn't let him in. Harry thought my father was simply an Irish drunk.

Harry and I rented a nice apartment on the East Side below Third Avenue. It was unfurnished so we had to go out and buy some furniture. We didn't decorate it or do very much with it as we didn't know how long we would be there. Early in the morning, Harry, who had been a musician, used to play for me while he was still in his bathrobe. Sometimes he would play 'Speak to Me of Love' to me on the violin or 'When Irish Eyes are Smiling' on the piano. He was really brilliant and incredibly romantic! We didn't go on a honeymoon straight away because Harry was busy working. He and his brother Eddie produced another movie, *Saint Benny the Dip*, with Dick Haymes, Nina Foch, and Lionel Stander – a comic thriller about a thief who poses as a Catholic priest.

I continued to work at modelling and fashion jobs for magazines. It was a very happy period for both of us. At the end of 1950, when the film was completed, Harry brought me on honeymoon to England on the *Queen Mary*. We celebrated the New Year on board the ship. When we disembarked in England there were photographers waiting for celebrities on the dock. As I came down the gangplank, the flashbulbs suddenly went off because the photographers thought I was Elizabeth Taylor!

12

Please Don't Call Me Elizabeth Taylor!

**NO, IT'S NOT—
ELIZABETH**

SHE'S a star in her own right, but film fans who mob her think she's Elizabeth Taylor, the British-born star. She's almost her double, but the name is Sheila Connolly, of American television, here to make, she hopes, a career in British pictures.

The next day the front page of every newspaper had a picture of me with the headline, 'Please do not call me Elizabeth Taylor!' - which I never said. Elizabeth Taylor was in London at the time with her fiancé, Michael Wilding. Harry and I were staying in the lap of luxury at the Savoy and the phone was ringing constantly with agents who wanted to represent me for acting. Eventually, I signed up with an agency called Routledge & White and Gordon White became my agent, but it was very difficult for an American to get work in London unless you were a star. We were invited to attend a party at Les Ambassadors and among the other guests were Liz Taylor and Michael Wilding. It was the first time I had seen her in person. We were introduced and politely said hello to each other but it was slightly unnerving!

After we had been in London a week or so, Harry told me that he and his brother Eddie were going on an extended business trip in preparation for their next film and that it would be too strenuous for me. I was a little disappointed but I just accepted it because I understood it was business. I was to remain in London and stay in a girls' club for budding young actresses, sponsored by Princess Marie Louise, called the Three Arts Club.

After Harry left I felt lost and alone and so I decided to take a trip to Ireland. It was hard because it was my first visit to Ireland since we had left for America. I went to visit Mama's grave but it was so overgrown I could hardly find it. That was even more distressing. I found it harrowing to go there on my own and it brought back some bad memories. I thought of Timmy and wished he were with me. Brownstown was exactly the same, except that some of the people I knew were gone: Mrs Higgins was dead and my friend Noeleen had moved away. I went into my friend Leila Doyle's shop and both she and her mother were there. They acted as though I had never been away. Leila said to her mother, 'Here's Sheila, how do you think she looks?' Her mother said, 'Well, she would look fine if she would get that muck off her face.' I was wearing a beaver fur coat and high heels but they never said another word to me about my appearance.

Sheila in Ireland, 1950

As my agent, Gordon White saw to it that I was invited to important events where I should be seen and which could be good PR for me. Whenever there was an important function on at Albert Hall or any other significant London venue, Gordon would invite me because he knew how lonely I was and how much I missed Harry. He was later knighted for his contribution to the arts and died in 1995.

Three months later, to my great surprise, the bold Harry arrived back just in time for my twenty-first birthday and we went to a command performance of the Royal Ballet's *Giselle*. The prima ballerina, Alicia Markova, was a friend of Harry. After the performance we went backstage and she gave me one of her ballet slippers, which she signed for me. Next I got the news that we were leaving London right away to go to Paris because Harry and Eddie were going to make a film in Barcelona and Harry needed to do some work first to get the script in order.

In Paris we stayed at the Hotel Matignon. After so many months apart, it was like a second honeymoon. Harry and I had great fun there. It was such an exciting place. The concierge was so funny – he knew everything about everyone and you just knew he was listening in on all your phone calls.

There were a lot of interesting people in Paris at that time – half of Hollywood, in fact. We had dinner with Sam Spiegel, who was making preparations for the production of *The African Queen* with Humphrey Bogart. Harry told him he was going to produce a movie in Barcelona with Gypsy Rose Lee (the most famous stripper in the world) and Paulette Goddard, who had been married to Charlie Chaplin. Sam Spiegel thought Paulette would be too

Sheila and Harry in Madrid, 1951

difficult but she was just great! We stayed in Paris a few months before departing for Spain, but my French was terrible. In one restaurant I proudly ordered butter: '*Du beurre, s'il vous plaît,*' and to my amusement, the waiter brought me two beers. I hoped my Spanish would be better!

One afternoon we were sitting outside a café drinking coffee in a sleepy little village near Paris when the director Roberto Rossellini was stopped by the police for speeding through in his Ferrari. The offence took place right in front of our café so he decided to stop and join us for a coffee. He was married to Ingrid Bergman at the time. I have to say I thought he was one of the most charming men I have ever met.

We drove down through France to Spain and were put up in Barcelona at the Ritz Hotel. It was very difficult to make a film in Spain at that time because of the repression of the Franco government. We had to pay a local Benedictine convent to help us to sneak in film negatives under a nun's habit! Gypsy and Paulette followed later. I loved Barcelona and the people who lived there, and I became especially interested in flamenco dancing. I found a great teacher, Trini Burull, who was a real gypsy dancer, and I made good progress with her. I even bought a real flamenco dancer's dress with a long train. One night at our favourite restaurant, El Canario, next to the Ritz, they were playing gypsy music. Everyone was encouraging me to dance, especially Gypsy Rose, so I got up on one of the tables and did a dance that my teacher had taught me. I got a standing ovation and the owner put my photograph permanently on his menu.

The restaurant at the Ritz was always interesting.

Paulette Goddard and Sheila chez Balenciaga

Sheila, Mario Cabre (bullfighter), Harry and Gypsy Rose Lee

Salvador Dali was staying in the hotel at the time and sat at the same table every day. He looked so strange, with that moustache which came to a sharp spike at each side. We thought he was absolutely crazy. His overcoat always hung loosely on his shoulders and he used to have a very interesting walking stick. One day while I was in the restaurant at lunch Mr Dali asked one of the waiters to tell me he would like to draw my picture. At the time I had no idea who Salvador Dali was and told the waiter to reply that I would think about it. Imagine! If only I had known who he was! Not surprisingly, I never heard from him again.

Harry and Eddie's film, *Babes in Baghdad*, was, of course, set in a harem. The budget was not big, so even though we all stayed at the Ritz I am sure we had a special arrangement because of all the people we had there. Harry and Eddie were putting up the money. Gypsy, Paulette and I became best friends. Paulette and Gypsy got along very well but had different interests. Gypsy and I liked to do

*Conrado San Martin, Gypsy Rose Lee and Sheila
in Montserrat, 1951*

a lot of sightseeing. I remember once going to Montserrat with her. She used to love to bring along five-year-old Eric, her son by Otto Preminger, a fact which she disclosed to her son only in her will after her death. He developed a big crush on me and insisted on going with me to my flamenco lessons. I used to try and sneak out of the hotel before he could find me but when Gypsy bought him a pair of flamenco dancing boots I didn't have the heart not to take him. Eric loved to wear a kilt; I felt a little embarrassed going with him dressed like this because some people in Barcelona would say what a cute little girl he was. He was a cute *boy*. Paulette also loved the high-fashion houses so we were constantly going to place like Balenciaga, where they would put on private showings for us. I found a few things that were fun, like a horsehair see-through overskirt! Gypsy especially loved a fashion shop called Pedrerol y Bofils and was always commissioning things to be made there.

Eventually the shooting of *Babes in Baghdad* began. John Boles, Richard Ney (who was married to Greer Garson) and Conrado San Martin, a Spanish actor, were added to the cast; I was one of the handmaidens. The director Edgar Ulmer was very difficult and he had a bad temper. He was very intimidating and I was terrified of him.

Mario Cabre, the famous bullfighter, was in Barcelona for a major bullfight at the time. He had just had a big love affair with Ava Gardner and had written and published a book of poems for her. We all became friends and he gave me a gift of the book, writing a nice inscription to me. I went to one of his bullfights but it revolted me.

Gypsy loved cats and she kept several Siamese in her

room at the hotel. I used to be afraid to go into her room because there was always one cat that would spring out of nowhere and cling on to my back. Gypsy would calmly say, 'Don't worry! He will eventually let go,' and when I would say, 'But when?' she would just laugh. The movie was taking much longer than anticipated, so when I met a photographer who did commercial work I started doing modelling for him and doing some advertisements as well. In spite of this I was getting lonely and homesick, and I missed my sisters and Timmy. I wanted to go back home to New York. I confided in Gypsy and she was very helpful. She asked me what I really wanted. I said I didn't know but I thought I would like to leave and maybe go to Hollywood.

I told Harry I was leaving and he said, 'Okay, if that's what will make you happy, I'll see you in New York.' Harry was working so hard that he didn't have time for anything, let alone our marriage. He had a lot on his mind at this point and a lot at stake, while having to cope with the actors' problems and schedules. I felt lonely and unproductive and needed to do *something*. I wanted to work. Harry understood this and would never have held me back. We were going our own way; I still loved Harry but we were both searching for what we wanted to do in life. I knew in my own mind that I wanted to be on my own.

13

MEETING THE STARS

When I arrived in New York from Spain I was overjoyed to see my sisters and Timmy again. We had a lot to talk about. Dolores was married with a son; Maureen was married with a son, Paddy was married, Joan had a boyfriend and Timmy and my father were working with horses in Maryland. I explained why I had decided to return home, and as usual they were very supportive. They just wanted me to be happy.

You have to bear in mind that I was still only twenty-two years old and had my whole life to lead. Harry was very good to me and supported me while I was building up my career. We wrote to each other every now and then. I kept really busy so I hadn't time to think. I moved into the Barbizon Girls' Rooming House, where a lot of the models lived at the time because it was a safe place for a single girl. A group of us still meet once a year. It's so funny because we all want to look our best and keep our looks and our figures. It's really nice that we are all still friends after all these years. One member of the group is Tippi Hedren, who was the female lead in Hitchcock's *The*

Birds and is Melanie Griffith's mother. I got to know her later in California and we found we shared friends from old Barbizon days. It was a very exciting time to be in New York and for the first time I really felt in control of my own destiny. I enrolled in a model agency again and quickly began doing commercials for Lux soap.

Then I got an interview for *The Jackie Gleason Show* and was offered a job as a straight girl. I used to introduce the items and do funny little skits. One of them was 'The Gun Moll'. I used to come on in high heels, and Jackie Gleason had a big long cigarette in his mouth. I was supposed to kiss him and of course the cigarette would break up. Then I was also offered the job as assistant on *The Winner Takes All*. I did both shows for a while, which gave me great exposure.

At night I used to love to listen to the radio before I fell asleep. My favourite station was WNEW. They had a request programme at midnight that I really loved which was presented by a man called Art Ford. He had a lovely deep, sonorous voice and played semi-classical music. I particularly loved Mantovani, whom Harry had introduced me to, and one night I called the station and made a request. 'I'm afraid I don't happen to have that right now,' Art said, 'but is there some other song you would like?' He asked me where I was from and I told him I was Sheila from Ireland. He asked me again if I had any particular song he could play for me. I told him how I loved the song 'When I Grow Too Old to Dream'. Then one night when I was listening to his programme he said he was going to dedicate the next song to me. 'This is for Sheila,' he said simply. Within seconds, I was transported back to the little kitchen in Brownstown, curled up on Mama's lap while she rocked me in her arms. I was so overcome when I heard the music that I cried. It was as if time stood still. I called and thanked him later and said it would be nice to meet him in person some time. He asked me if I would like to come to a party that weekend. It was being hosted at The Little Club, a popular nightclub in New York.

There were lots of famous people there, like the singer Eddie Fisher, who was still a bachelor, and Bobby Short, a well-known entertainer in New York at that time. However, it was my old acquaintance George Shearing who utterly captivated me and with whom I spent most of the evening talking about Ireland. Art Ford was very nice and introduced me to everyone so that when he had to leave for his show, I felt content about staying on at the party on my own.

It was snowing when it was time for me to go home. Just as I was heading out the door Mike Todd offered me a lift. He was the producer who made the film *Around the World in Eighty Days* in 1956. The scene was like something out of the movies. Out of the swirling snowflakes came the yellow lights of his Rolls-Royce. It stopped outside the door. As I went down the steps his chauffeur jumped out of the car with an umbrella and opened the car door for me. I caught the smell of leather seats and cigar smoke. It was like entering a gentleman's club. Mike Todd's gruff manner scared me a little so I sat way over in the far corner of the car. He looked me up and down as he puffed on his big cigar. I must have looked frightened because he turned to me with a little smile and said, 'Don't worry, kid! You're too skinny for me.' With that he exhaled a cloud of smoke. On the journey home he looked as if his mind was far away and when I got out of the car he said, 'Have a good night, kid!' before disappearing into the night. Later Mike married Elizabeth Taylor.

I got to know Eddie Fisher as well. He married a good friend of mine, Debbie Reynolds. Eddie and Mike Todd were close friends, so much so, in fact, that when Mike was killed in a plane crash in 1958, Eddie Fisher became a great friend to Elizabeth Taylor and they fell in love. When Eddie met Elizabeth he was still married to Debbie Reynolds and she'd just given birth to their second baby. However, he fell so much in love with Elizabeth that he divorced Debbie straight away; it shattered her. She threw herself into her work, accepting the lead in a film in Europe starring Glenn Ford. She later wrote to me from France saying how much she missed her children.

After a few months of working in New York, I decided it was time to leave for Hollywood. So I set off on my own. Looking back, I think if I hadn't been so young I might not have felt so brave. It was a big step for a girl from Brownstown to go it alone in Hollywood but I knew I needed to keep moving if I was to realise my full career potential. I really wanted to break into movies.

Fortunately for me, before I left for California Gypsy Rose Lee had sent a letter to her sister June Havoc, a well-known actress, who had kindly given me some letters of introduction to friends of hers in Hollywood who would see that I got invited to things. June had also given me professional letters of introduction and phone numbers and the name of the casting director in Columbia, Abner Biberman.

I checked into a little hotel called the Beverly Carlton on Olympic Boulevard in Beverly Hills which had been wisely recommended to me by June. It was such a friendly place – a lot of actors, actresses and musical dancers stayed there. I met the well-known choreographer Bob Fosse from Broadway while we were relaxing around the pool. Marilyn Monroe was also staying there at the time and was dating Joe DiMaggio. We all got to know each other pretty well. Like all Californian hotels, it was built in a circle, and it didn't really have a restaurant. Since I was staying there indefinitely the manager moved me to the annexe just across the street; the annexe had a small kitchen and was more convenient for me.

After a while I decided it was time to move out of the Beverly Carlton and I took a little apartment in Hollywood on a bus route to the studios – useful because I didn't drive. I loved the town, the people and the sunshine and had made many friends. I built up a whole new way of life there. Because of my childhood I was a tough kid, very adaptable, and I knew I could go it alone. Hollywood was the first place I had ever really felt at home. I felt enormously confident as a result. I was also starting to get some television work acting with people like Broderick Crawford and Edmund Gwenn, the star of the original *Miracle on 34th Street,* and went for an interview to meet Alfred Hitchcock. He asked me if Elizabeth Taylor knew I was around, to which I innocently replied that she did!

Just before I moved out of the Beverly Carlton, I wrote to Harry in Spain and told him I wanted a divorce. When we parted in Barcelona neither of us was sure what would happen to us. Now I knew it was no use; we were going in opposite directions. Harry flew out to California and we talked. We were very sorry and we were still good friends, but on different routes. For me it was Hollywood, for Harry it was Europe. He and his brother foresaw that Europe was the direction in which the movie industry was heading. Harry and I leased a car, drove to Tijuana, Mexico, and filed for divorce. He tried to talk me out of it even while we were there. We spent the night together and the next day parted sadly but on very good terms.

It was essentially a question of timing. I think Harry and I were right for each other but we married at the wrong time. Little did I know that one day our paths would cross again.

At the beginning of 1953, I called Arthur Loew, who was part of the MGM family and worked as a young executive at MGM studios. I told him that I'd been given Dick Carroll's number to call. Dick Carroll had the most important men's clothing store in Beverly Hills, and still does. The clothes are imports from England. Dick and Arthur shared a house but when I phoned him he was out of town. Arthur was very kind to me and we became good friends. He introduced me to a lot of studio people. Unfortunately, where MGM was concerned, I was too like Elizabeth Taylor, whom they had on their books. It was a nice complaint, I guess.

One night, Arthur invited me to an amazing party which was given by Marion Davies, who owned Falcon's Lair, the old Valentino home in Beverly Hills. Marion Davies was the girlfriend of the newspaper mogul William Randolph Hearst. For the party, every room had been transformed into a replica of a famous nightclub from around the world, such as Maxim's, the Casbah etc. It was *the* party of the year. Every big star in Hollywood came, from Lana Turner to Fernando Lamas, from Ava Gardner to Frank Sinatra. I wore a long white strapless gown with a full skirt of tulle; the bodice was made of white iridescent sequins with a matching stole. Arthur had insisted on buying it for me – it was very expensive. Arthur always dressed in very well-cut suits from Carroll & Co, Dick's men's clothing store in Beverly Hills.

We continued to see each other regularly. Arthur had just broken up with the actress Janet Leigh, the star of *Psycho*. He was a real fun-loving person; he loved comedy and I was a good audience; he loved parties and so did I. One night I decided to cook dinner at his house for some of his friends. I didn't know how to cook but I was sure I could make spaghetti. I might have been a little over-ambitious. The spaghetti was boiling over on to the stove because I had put too much in the saucepan. I had to keep taking out mounds of pasta when it got too full. Then I casually poured a whole bottle of spicy Tabasco into the tomato sauce to liven it up. It was like an episode out of *The Lucy Show*. I nearly killed everyone with the hot sauce. Arthur thought it was the funniest evening he had ever had but I was very embarrassed.

After seeing each other for months we knew that neither of us wanted to get married. When we broke up we stayed good friends. He later married Tyrone Powers's widow, Debbie.

I met Donald O'Connor for the first time with Gene Kelly and Debbie Reynolds at a party in Hollywood before

Donald O'Connor and Sheila skiing in Mammoth, 1953

he made the musical *Singing in the Rain*. At the time, Donald had his own TV variety show. He was a talented dancer, singer, actor and comedian. On a personal level, he was very funny and sensitive. He invited me to meet some old friends of his, Judy Garland and her husband, Sid Luft, for dinner. We were going to meet at the Villa Nova, a very popular Italian restaurant on Sunset Boulevard.

Donald and Judy had known each other since they were very young and both had worked on the stage, though not together. They spent the whole evening reminiscing about their childhood. It was very poignant when Judy asked Donald in a childlike voice, 'Were you happy, Donald?' and he answered that he wasn't. I sat there in mesmerised silence. Then Judy said, 'What about you, Sheila, what was your childhood like?' When I described briefly to them how it had been, Judy remarked that Oliver Twist had had it good, compared to me! We were all a little misty-eyed during that dinner.

Donald and I became good friends and we would go skiing together now and then. Through Donald and Arthur, I met Debbie Reynolds. She invited me to her home in Burbank to meet her parents. Her mother was wonderful to me – and still is. To this day she refers to me as one of her daughters. We are very close.

I continued to work on my career in both acting and modelling. I interviewed for a modelling job at the Paul Hesse and Wally Seawell photographic studios. Wally Seawell was well known for photographing the stars and members of high society. He has photographed President Johnson, President and Nancy Reagan, Doris Duke,

Barbara Hutton, the Duke and Duchess of Windsor and the King and Queen of Siam. Paul was also a prominent photographer; he did all the layouts for stars for Howard Hughes. One day, while I was at the studio, Wally said he wanted me to meet someone and took me to the big office at the back of his studio. Inside there was a very tall man sitting in a barber's chair getting a shave and a manicure. Wally took me by the hand and led me over to him, saying, 'Mr Hughes, this is Sheila Connolly from Ireland and Sheila, this is Howard Hughes.' Well, believe it or not, I had no idea who Howard Hughes was. He asked me did I want to be an actress and I said I did. Howard looked at Wally and asked him to do a photo-lay on me. As I was led out of the room I asked Wally who that was and he was a little upset with me. 'He's only one of the most famous people in the world,' he said, sarcastically, and when I asked what he was famous for, he just looked at me and shook his head.

As I was leaving, Wally asked me to be in the studio the next morning and asked whether I would like to go to a party that night for Greg Bautzer. When I asked who Greg was, Wally just rolled his eyes again and said, 'Never mind!' Greg Bautzer, he explained, was attorney to Howard Hughes and the stars and a very well-known man about town. Needless to say, I went to the party! And Wally gave me a superb photo-lay.

Wally and I became friends. He was a great dancer and since I liked to dance he used to invite me to lots of parties and social events. Parties were very big in those days. One evening he invited me to a party at the Whitney home, a real high-society establishment, where I met a young man named Lance Reventlow. I recognised him from Wally's photographs of him, but once again I did not know who he actually was.

What I did know was that he was tall and blonde, with brown eyes and dimples, and extremely handsome and charming. As I was chatting to him I told him how my first job in America was with Woolworth's and he seemed to think that was very funny. I realised later that he was the son of Barbara Hutton, the Woolworth heiress, and Count Court Haugwitz Reventlow. He was very sophisticated for his age. Lance and I got along really well and spent the whole evening talking about ourselves.

Lance wanted to take me out on a date but I hesitated when I found out that he was seventeen, whereas I was a mature twenty-three. Every time I opened my door he was sitting there on the ground waiting for me, begging me for a date. Eventually I relented; the next time I found Lance camped outside my apartment I agreed to meet him for one drink. I had no intention of getting involved with Lance, although he had a really good sense of humour and looked much older then he was. We went to the Polo Lounge in the Beverly Hills Hotel. He was also a practical joker and had arranged that the bar staff would question my age when I ordered a Dubonnet on ice and Lance ordered a gin and tonic. The waiter asked me for ID, which I didn't have, but didn't ask Lance for any. I was slightly put out. So he ended up serving Lance his drink but wouldn't serve me. Then Lance started to laugh and told me it was all a joke: his drink was ginger ale, not gin and tonic.

That's how our friendship began. I thought Lance was

The wedding of Barbara Hutton and Cary Grant

a lot of fun but I would never want to be seriously involved with him. He told me how his father had taken him away from his mother shortly after his parents' divorce. His mother had just married Cary Grant and his father had obviously been very upset about the custody arrangements. Lance was only seven at the time and didn't see his mother until he was fourteen. He suffered from asthma and was sent to school in Arizona because of its dry climate. Later on his mother divorced Cary Grant, though they remained friends. Lance remained very fond of Cary and his new wife, Betsy Drake.

Lance and I used regularly to go up to Cary and Betsy's house in Beverly Hills. When I discovered one day that Betsy was a good guitarist I asked her to give me lessons. She gave me a lesson there and then and taught me to play a little tune. I'd always wanted to play a musical instrument. Her pet name for Lance was 'Little Spear'. They took us out to dinner at Chasens restaurant, famous for attracting the stars, and we dined with the author Sidney Sheldon and his wife, Jorja.

Lance was very close to Bill Robertson, his mother's confidante and close friend. He lived in the Hollywood hills and kept an eye on Lance, often having us up to visit. I really liked Bill and we became very close friends. Lance and I used to cook for ourselves. Lance loved to make me fluffy omelettes and was very proud of his cooking prowess. He often cooked for me in Bill's home. He liked going to Bill's because he felt so much at home there; there weren't servants about so he was able to relax.

He had to go back to Arizona to his exclusive school for his graduation ceremony and sent me an engraved invitation to come. I declined because I felt it was inappropriate. He was upset as a result. Bill Robertson and Cary Grant went but when Barbara, his mother, didn't show, he became very upset and lashed out at Bill and Cary, taking his hurt out on them. His mother had fallen ill at the last minute and couldn't travel.

When Lance came back to California he told me his mother wanted him to come to Europe for the summer but he didn't want to go – he wanted to stay with me. I said that I was too old for him and that he should go to his mother. Bill and I put him on a plane. He looked vulnerable and forlorn, lugging a big oxygen tank for his asthma behind him. He gave me a photo of himself on which he had inscribed, *'Pour Sheila, avec tout mon amour et mon coeur. A bientôt! Lance.'*

Barbara called Cary and asked him why Lance hadn't wanted to come to Europe. Cary told her that he was in love with an Irish girl; so Barbara asked Cary if he thought I would go too. Cary asked me, telling me that I would love Barbara and really should go. So, after speaking with Bill Robertson, I decided that I would follow Lance and was sent first-class tickets on TWA with a sleeping compartment to New York, where I changed planes for Paris.

14

I DANCED WITH A PRINCE!

When I arrived in Paris, Lance met me at the plane with his governess Tiki, who had been Barbara's governess when she was a child. Barbara's mother had committed suicide when she was very young so Tiki was almost like a mother to her. We got into a chauffeur-driven limousine with two dozen white roses on the seat. Lance handed me a box from Cartier's which contained a pair of earrings – dropped opal hearts – which he had had remodelled from his grandfather's cufflinks. I was very touched by this gesture. Tiki and Lance took me to my room at the Ritz and we met his mother Barbara for dinner. Oh, I loved staying at the Ritz!

The next day Barbara asked to see me in her suite, where I found her in bed, looking stunning in white silk pyjamas with her blonde hair pulled back. She had the most amazing translucent blue eyes. She was a real natural beauty. She told me to go over to the chest of drawers, open the top drawer and help myself to half a dozen Hermes scarves. And I was so stupid at the time, I told her politely that I didn't wear scarves. It never occurred to me that I might in time grow to like them! So she got out of bed, went over towards the wardrobe and pulled out a sable stole which she handed to me. 'Well, you will wear this,' she said. Then she gave me a beautiful crocodile purse. She was the most generous person I have ever encountered. She just showered her friends with gifts. I felt overwhelmed and a little uncomfortable. It gave me a strange kind of empty feeling and I didn't understand why I didn't feel happy.

She asked me what I thought of Lance and I told her I thought he was a lot of fun and that he was very proud of her from the way he spoke. I was totally straight with her and explained that I was not in love with Lance. I reassured her that I cared deeply for him and that we were good friends. After I left her room Lance and I got some balloons, filled them with water and dropped them from the first-floor balcony down into the garden restaurant. The manager reported this to Barbara and threatened to put us out of the hotel if we ever did anything like that again. Barbara was amused.

We went to some fun places and restaurants. There was one little restaurant called Mouton de la Panache, which was up a little stairway, where there was a live sheep walking around with a basket of flowers on its back so that you could help yourself to one of them. When bread rolls were brought to the table, all the women in the restaurant would scream when they saw them since they were in the shape of a penis and testicles. Every night a different guest was picked for the 'garter of honour', and the night we were there, Barbara was selected. The ritual was that you had to stand on a chair and put your leg on the table so that the waiter could slip the garter on your thigh. Luckily Barbara was a really good sport! Cary Grant was right: she *was* wonderful.

Another night we went to a piano bar with Lance's notorious cousin Jimmy Donahue. There was talk in the inner circles, Lance told me, that Jimmy and the Duchess of Windsor were more than close, because she often visited him at his suite in the Ritz and on his bedside table was a picture of her with an endearing inscription. I'm sure the Duke of Windsor suspected that this was going on. But, you know, he adored Wallis.

While we were at the piano bar Jimmy casually got up from the table and danced around the room and started to remove every stitch of his clothing. And then when he was finished he just put his clothes back on as if nothing had happened. Lance laughed heartily at this and seemed used to such behaviour.

The next day we were told we were going to the Duchess of Windsor's birthday party with Barbara. It was being held at the home of the duke and duchess in the Bois de Boulogne. When we arrived, Barbara presented us to the duke and duchess. We were served an aperitif and hors d'oeuvres. In the dining room the tables were all in a circle and the centre was a dance floor. I remember I wore a short white strapless dress in *peau de soie* but I didn't have the right shoes to go with it. All I had were the black suede pumps which were de rigueur for models at that time. And I wore the new earrings Lance had given me.

Barbara wanted us to have the experience of sitting beside the duke and duchess. So at one stage of the night

Lance sat on the duchess's right and I sat on the left of the duke. People have always asked me if I thought he regretted what he had given up for her. I don't think he wanted to be king. The duchess was so warm and alive, and she made us feel incredibly welcome. She had a wonderful smile. She told me what a charming boy Lance was and I agreed.

The duchess asked Lance to dance and then the duke made the same request of me. I was so nervous I kept stepping all over his shoes. When I apologised he was very polite and said modestly that he was not a good dancer, whereas in reality he was very accomplished and quite adorable. He asked me where I was from and I told him the Curragh, County Kildare. 'Oh yes, I know the Curragh; my father, King George, often went to the military camp there.' The duke was very interested in the fact that my grandfather Thornton was a merchant and used to supply all the food and crested dinnerware for King George on his visits to the Curragh. He was amazed at the coincidence, and when the dance ended he thanked me and made a slight bow.

Then we changed partners. It was the kind of dinner party where you changed partners with different courses. At the end of the evening, the duke gave me a little ashtray made of Limoges china from the table. It had an inscription in French which, roughly translated, meant, 'Three daughters with the mother are four devils for the father.'

When I got back to my hotel room that night I decided that I wanted to go home. I felt totally out of my depth in these opulent surroundings and in this social circle. The next day I told Lance that I wanted to go back to

California. The party was going on to Tangiers and Barbara had invited me to join them. He pleaded with me to go on to Tangiers with them but I had made up my mind to leave. I'd had enough.

On my last night Lance and I went to dinner at a Russian club with Bill Robertson. Bill and I were sitting in a booth against the wall, with Lance facing us. During the course of the evening Bill suddenly grabbed his trouser leg at his thigh and began struggling with something. And I thought, my God what's he doing. When I looked at his face I thought for a minute he was having a seizure; he had turned so white and kept squeezing his trouser leg really hard. Then he stood up and shook his leg. Suddenly a big rat fell down on the floor – it was either dead or unconscious from Bill's squeezing it. The worst thing was that the waiter came over calmly, picked the stunned rat up, put it on a plate and calmly walked away. I felt sick at the sight. No doubt he returned the house speciality to the chef! They said that our dinner would be on the house but somehow we weren't very hungry.

The next day I went to say goodbye to Barbara and thank her. She said she realised Lance was very young but that she would like to see him with someone like me. She handed me a little box and inside was a Cartier pin in the shape of a shamrock. The centrepiece was an emerald and it was surrounded by diamonds. Lance took me to the airport and we promised to always remain friends.

A few months later, when Lance returned to California, he tracked me down even though I had moved to another apartment. He was taking flying lessons and had bought

Pour Sheila mon amour
Avec tout ce qui
et mon bien amour
à bien[?]

a small plane. He asked me if I would like to go up for a spin in his plane and I bravely agreed to go. I would have tried anything in those days. We flew from Burbank airport along the coast from Malibu up to Santa Barbara to have lunch, then flew back to Los Angeles that evening. After that I didn't see him for some time. Then one day I read in the paper he was going to marry the actress Jill St John. I did see him again in a restaurant one night shortly after he had married Jill. (Sadly, that marriage ended in divorce.) Lance was killed in a small plane which crashed in Aspen, Colorado, in 1972. Only the good die young.

15

KOREA

Just before Christmas 1953, I found out about a USO (Combat Entertainers) show going over to Korea to visit the US troops. Johnny Grant - a comedian and Hollywood's ambassador of goodwill to the world - was heading the troupe. He was the unofficial mayor of Hollywood and officiated at all the ceremonies when big stars had their footprints put on the Hollywood Walk of Fame. I really wanted to go on that Korean trip and contacted Johnny. He said they had enough people, that the plane was full. I persisted, and in the end, after all my pleas, he asked me what I could do. He thought he might be able to use me as his 'straight girl': I could throw him the lines and he would come back with wisecracks. I also said I could sing. Finally, he said OK and told me I would have to get all my shots before travelling, then file for my army ID.

He warned me that if there was an emergency alert during my stay there I would have to fend for myself and also advised me that it was bitterly cold over there. The army would issue me with heavy-duty army clothing but for the stage I'd need to bring nice warm performing clothes. I knew Debbie Reynolds had already gone on a tour there, so I contacted her and asked if I could borrow some stage clothes. She lent me some pretty quilted skirts and her mother lent me some attractive sweaters. In fact, Debbie Reynolds had asked me to spend Christmas with them.

One morning, before I left for Korea, I was in a drugstore near my apartment. I was approached by a man who told me a friend of his was making a Western movie and he thought I would be perfect for the lead. He gave me the telephone number and said to call right away. Not taking it seriously, I didn't call, but the next day he came back looking for me in the drugstore. He was annoyed that I hadn't phoned because they were expecting my call. I did call and was asked to come in for an interview. They liked me and set up a film test the next day. The test appeared to go very well, although I didn't hear from them before I left for Korea. I also found out that the man who had seen me at the drugstore was a producer named Milton Bren, who was married to the famous actress Claire Trevor.

On 21 December we all met at the army plane which was going to take us to Japan and then on to Korea. I was very excited about the tour. While we were stopped over in Hawaii for refuelling I went into a little coffee shop. I remember hearing Bing Crosby's voice on the radio singing 'White Christmas' and I suddenly felt nostalgic and lonely for Harry. I had once met Bing Crosby through a girl I knew who worked in his office. Her name was Leis and when she told him she had met a girl from Ireland who was dying to meet him, he was curious to meet me. So she invited him around to the apartment for lunch. We made hamburgers for him but he didn't eat anything! That was probably a wise move on his part!

From Hawaii we flew on towards Japan and stopped on the beautiful Midway Island to refuel again. There we saw hundreds of albatross (gooneybirds, as the Americans called them). The amazing thing about these birds is when they walk, their heads bob up and down. It was really funny to watch hundreds of them in similar motion. The scenery was pretty staggering too.

When we finally arrived in Tokyo, we were driven to the Imperial Hotel for what was to be our last night of luxury. My room-mate was Merry Anders, a beautiful blonde Marilyn Monroe type who was one of the nicest girls I have ever known. Next day, we left for Korea, transported from the airport to our camp by helicopters. During the course of the flight the door of our helicopter suddenly flew off in mid-air. The pilot was very casual and said not to worry, so I didn't! I was too riveted by the sight of snow-capped mountains and bare rugged landscapes seen from the air. And as you can imagine, it was pretty cold at this high altitude, with icy air billowing through the cabin.

To my delight, in Korea, Merry and I were room-mates again and I was happy because we got along so well. She nicknamed me 'little bird'. Our names were printed on cardboard and placed on our door with a star. Merry got top billing and I was next. Sometimes we played a trick on each other and switched our names around. We slept in bunks with sleeping bags, housed in the same kind of billets

Sheila and Johnny Grant in Korea

Sheila with an orphan boy in Korea

as the soldiers. We had no shower facilities, just wash basins. It was all pretty basic. Most of all, it was cold.

I was lying in my bunk the first night we were there when I heard some beautiful choral singing. I put on my heavy army-issue jacket and went outside, following the sound. It was snowing very hard and freezing cold but I couldn't help thinking, even though it was a war zone, how beautiful it looked. It was like a Christmas card. Suddenly I missed Timmy and my sisters. I came upon the soldiers' little makeshift church and quietly slipped inside so as not to disturb anyone. The choir was composed of a group of young soldiers who, when they saw me, immediately stopped singing. For a minute, they said, they thought I was an angel. They didn't know the USO group had arrived. They all started crying and so did I. It was such an emotional occasion that I will never forget it.

The next day we started doing the shows. The hundreds of soldiers sitting on the cold ground were a wonderful audience because they loved everything and anything we did – they were so glad to see us. Johnny organised the shows and we had musicians with us. There was an outdoor set-up stage that the soldiers had built for us. It was freezing cold. I had never experienced anything like it in my life and it made it very hard to perform. We wore heavy sweaters when we went out on the stage.

It was a variety show. Penny Singleton, who was well known as Blondie from her series of movies *The Bumpsteads*, based on the syndicated comic strip, was the singer. The soldiers loved Penny and she was so kind to me – referring to me as her adopted daughter. She's in her nineties now and I still see her from time to time. She's wonderful. Marilyn Monroe was not with the tour but was there to help boost troop morale, and the soldiers loved her. She was great fun to be with and so warm and outgoing.

Colonel Reid and Marilyn Monroe

There was a great medley of stars. Terry Moore (rumoured to be Howard Hughes's wife) was the star of the show and she would go out and talk to the soldiers. Roberta Haynes, who starred in *Return to Paradise* with Gary Cooper, was there, as was Susan Zanuck, the daughter of Darryl. I used to have lines like, 'Gee, Johnny, you smell so nice! What's that aftershave you're using?' Johnny would reply 'Dirty Socks!' The troops loved it.

One camp we went to was on a very steep hill which during the show was covered in a splash of khaki from the soldiers' uniforms. And right at the top of the hill were the North Korean enemy, also watching the show, with their rifles resting on the ground. Sometimes we had to wear our helmets when we were in a really dangerous zone but none of us ever felt in danger. We moved around to different camps. Some of the soldiers wanted us to go to a hospital where there were badly injured personnel. It was in a very dangerous area which was off-limits to us. We decided to risk it. One of the boys took us in an ambulance, which was strictly against the rules, but afterwards we were very glad that we had gone. This was a makeshift hospital and conditions weren't exactly nice. The soldiers were so very badly wounded that we moved around their beds, sitting with them, talking to them and agreeing to take letters home to their loved ones for them. It was tragic to see so many injured and maimed young men.

The driver got into a lot of trouble and so did we; they almost sent us back. They told us that if there had been an alert when we were there we could have found ourselves in a very messy situation and they would have had

The Department of Defense

presents this

Certificate of Esteem

to

Sheila Connolly

for Patriotic Service in providing Entertainment
to Members of the Armed Forces in

Korea-Japan

during the period

1953 - 1954

Washington, D. C.

C. E. Wilson
_____
Secretary of Defense

[CERTIFICATE of APPRECIATION]

TO: SHELIA CONNOLLY

We wish to thank you for giving so much to American Soldiers here in Korea.

Traveling in a combat zone under field conditions has required you to perform in extreme heat or cold and under always difficult circumstances.

That you have won the unconditional acclaim of all Officers and Enlisted men of this command is a tribute both to your devotion to the American way of life and to your very fine artistic ability.

On behalf of all members of X Corp, let this certificate of appreciation serve as a heartfelt – _Thank you._

OFFICERS & MEN of the **BIG X CORP**

KOREA 1953

(signature)

SPECIAL SERVICES OFFICER

SPECIAL ☒ **SERVICES**

to abandon us. We had really disobeyed the rules. Of course, we appealed and apologised and said that we wouldn't do it again, although we were glad that we had gone because it had made so many of the soldiers happy. It was a great feeling to know that we really had made a difference and brightened up an otherwise very gloomy Christmas for these young troops who were so far away from their families and friends.

On Christmas Day Cardinal Spellman from the New York diocese came and said Mass. Afterwards we ate dinner with the soldiers, who made their own menu, with a lovely drawing of a snow scene. One of them gave me a lovely picture album for all the photos the soldiers took of us. I made this the basis of my Korean scrapbook. When our tour came to an end we were all sad and a lot of the soldiers cried openly, thanking us for coming because it meant such a lot to them. It meant a lot to us too and we were very grateful for the experience. I sometimes wonder what became of the soldiers. Some of them were just kids, so very young.

On the journey home we stopped off in Japan for a couple of days to do some shopping. At that time we all wanted cashmere polo coats. They had the most wonderful cashmere in Japan and it only cost $50 to have a full-length cashmere coat made. I had my heart set on a white cashmere coat. I thought it would be so luxurious. None of us had any money because we hadn't needed any on the tour. Then I remembered the name of the contact person that Cary Grant told me to look up in case I was in any kind of trouble, Walter Bouillet of Special Services. Walter insisted on lending us money to go shopping. I got a letter from him upon my return thanking us for the show and sending his regards to Cary. He also said that Cary always sent him the nicest people.

When we returned home we were all invited to a special dinner given by General J. Lemnitzer and were presented with medals. It was one of the proudest moments of my life.

16

GUY MADISON, ALIAS WILD BILL HICKOCK

To my absolute astonishment, when I returned from Korea, I was notified by my agent that not only had I got a part in a movie but that I was, in fact, the lead. The movie was called *The Outlaw's Daughter* and was going to be filmed on location in Sedona, Arizona. It just goes to show; it *is* a question of being in the right place at the right time.

One of the prerequisites for the part was that I could ride a horse. I would have to do a lot of rough riding over rocky terrain. I immediately went to a riding ranch and hired a man to give me lessons. I went every day and worked hard, jumping over rocks and galloping fast. I was really enjoying it and found it quite a challenge. By the time we left for Arizona I was getting very good at handling a horse. My co-stars were Jim Davis (later Jock Ewing in *Dallas*) and Bill Williams, star of a Western TV series called *Adventures of Kit Carson*.

For my costume, I wore a suede culotte skirt with a fringe and a short-sleeved top, laced up at the bust. This was teamed with a cowboy brown hat and boots. Arizona

Sheila (Kelly Ryan) with Bill Williams in The Outlaw's Daughter

was very beautiful and full of green prairies. We stayed at a little motel near the location site.

In order to keep up my horse-riding practice, I rode out to the location every day, galloping alongside the station wagons that carried the actors and the crew. I did all my own riding and didn't have a stunt girl because it was a low-budget film. There were some dangerous scenes, like when we were trying to get away from a robbery or something and Bill Williams would gallop past and whisk me off the ground and throw me over his saddle. Bill got worried about my getting hurt and warned the director about this.

We worked long hours under the same tough man and it was very exhausting. You didn't dare fluff your lines because he would get really angry. One day Bill Williams and I were feeling very giddy and every time the director said 'Roll it', we could get no further than the first line, when for some reason we would both burst into fits of giggles and wouldn't be able to stop. Finally the director became so upset that he said we were finished for the day. When we came back to the motel he came to my room and told me off, calling me unprofessional. I burst into tears and said it wouldn't happen again, although the next day I still had a hard time trying to keep a straight face.

I remember that when we returned to Los Angeles to do the interior shots, we were behind schedule. We ended up having to stay very late at night. I remember working very hard and being extremely tired. One night when they didn't need me I went to the dressing room, lay down and went to sleep. When they came back to the dressing room and woke me up to redo a scene, I broke down and cried with exhaustion. Everyone was just so tired. At the end of the film, I just slept and slept.

Finally we finished the picture and I felt very excited – that is until I found out they were changing my billing name on the credits to 'Kelly Ryan'. The producer didn't think Sheila Connolly was Irish enough! To me Kelly Ryan sounded like an American version of an Irish name. No one would know who Kelly Ryan was, so as you can imagine I was quite upset. But there was nothing I could do. I certainly had no intention of changing my name to Kelly Ryan after being Sheila Connolly for twenty-three years.

After the film, I worked on different TV shows such as *Highway Patrol*, with Broderick Crawford, and *Fireside Theatre*. Then entirely by chance I met a girl called Barbara who was handling the publicity for a boat show.

John Wayne, Sheila, Lawrence Harvey, Ronnie Cowan

She asked me if I would like to join her. Although I am not particularly interested in boats, I agreed. It was a big show and there were lots of celebrities attending. Someone asked me if I would pose for a photo in one of the craft for the newspaper. I had trouble getting on to the boat and an actor by the name of Guy Madison (alias Robert Moseley) offered to help. He picked me up into his arms to carry me over and at that moment the photographer snapped the picture which was to appear in the paper the very next day.

After the show there was a private party in the back of the auditorium, to which we were invited. Guy was there and asked me to sit at his table. He was extremely handsome in a very masculine kind of way and I didn't think I liked him. Maybe I should have trusted my initial gut instincts. However, when he asked if he could drive me home after the party I found myself agreeing. In the car he asked me about myself and I told him about my first movie and how they had changed my name. 'Yeah, that's show business for you!' he quipped.

He was working very hard on the well-known western TV series *Wild Bill Hickock* (sponsored by Kellogg's cereals) and he did not get much time off. Guy was Wild Bill Hickock himself, lawman and good guy, while Jingles was his sidekick. When he dropped me off he asked me for my telephone number, which I gave him. He told me how he loved fishing and said maybe I might like to go some morning. I told him I had never fished but he said I would love it. Strangely, he didn't call me for a while. In the meantime, I read in the newspapers that Guy was trying to get a divorce from the actress Gail Russell, who was a

Movie gal Gail Russell, whose cocktail capers have repeatedly gotten her in bad with Coast police, was given an ultimatum from her estranged husband, cowboy actor Guy Madison, that she either go through with a divorce or he'll bring suit. She's due to appear in court Wednesday. A settlement gives Gail $750 monthly, her home and car. Guy's been dating Sheila Connolly, brunette starlet from New York. (Mirror Photo)

dark-haired, almost purple-eyed beauty. According to the article, Gail had a drink problem.

Then one day the phone rang and a deep voice said, 'Pick you up at six am. We're going fishing,' and just hung up. It was Guy! The following day I was waiting, wearing blue jeans and a white cotton shirt, when he drove up in a new Lincoln. 'Good morning, bright eyes,' he said, and we drove off to Santa Monica, with his sixteen-foot boat hitched on to the back of a trailer. He backed the trailer on the beach with all the fishing gear in the boat and pulled it into the water. Off we went out into the ocean, quite far out, it seemed.

Then he turned the motor off and I started feeling a little queasy in the choppy water. Guy fixed the rods with bait and was about to hand me mine when I hung over the boat and was sick. I thought, how unromantic, but it didn't seem to bother him. Oh, it was so embarrassing! When I had finished throwing up, he calmly gave me my rod and we waited. Suddenly my line was pulling very hard and I had caught a fish, which appeared to be a good size.

I got worried because this was all so new to me. When I saw this big fish jumping out of the water on the end of a line I worried about how to get it into the boat. In my nervousness my Irish accent came out as I said, 'Oh, will it be splashing about in the boat?' Guy thought this was so funny that he collapsed into convulsions of laughter. He was laughing at my accent and the look on my face. And in later years, he used to recall this incident as a joke. We reeled in my first fish and put it in a bucket. After catching several more nice-sized fish, Guy said we'd finish up and suggested that we go back to his apartment, where he would clean the fish and cook me lunch.

Guy was a very tall, handsome man. He had a gruff way of expressing himself but I felt that was his way of not showing his emotions – it would be a sign of weakness for him to do that. He never said anything about Gail Russell during that first date; nor did I. When I got out of the car he said, 'I like your honesty. When you told me your father was a jockey, you could have said he was a big racehorse trainer – that's what most girls here would say.' It made me see that I should never need to lie about anything in my life.

I had never seen Guy's apartment before. I was expecting it to be a typical movie star's apartment and was surprised to see that all it seemed to contain was gym equipment, a workout bench, bows and arrows (he loved archery and made his own arrows) and fishing equipment.

It was obvious he was a real outdoors man. As a joke I used to describe the apartment decor as 'decorated early barbells'.

Guy left town when *The Wild Bill Hickock* show went on location and I didn't hear from him for some time. When he got back he called me and invited me to the house of his best friend, Howard Hill. Howard was one of the most famous archers in the world and made many trips to Africa to hunt wild animals. I told Guy I didn't approve of killing animals for sport but he said he only killed what he ate and he particularly loved venison – he said he would cook some for me one day. I was speechless with horror.

First, though, I decided to cook dinner for him, since he didn't seem to enjoy going out very much. I bought a leg of lamb and since I had never cooked one before I phoned Debbie Reynolds's mother Maxene, who told me to make little slits in the joint with a knife and stick cloves in the slits, then put mustard all over it. I thought she meant spiced cloves, whereas in fact she meant cloves of garlic. When I put the leg of lamb out for dinner, Guy asked what were in all the little holes. When I told him they were cloves, he said it must be the way they do it in Ireland. I said it was but soon realised something wasn't right. He ate it anyway and politely said it tasted different.

We saw each other often and he finally told me he was trying to get a divorce but that Gail's drinking problem meant that she wouldn't sign the papers. The thought of the break-up contributed to her feelings of self-loathing and other symptoms. Guy wasn't very sympathetic. He used to call her the drunk in spite of my asking him not

DAILY MIRROR TUESDAY OCTOBER 26 1954

Actor Guy Madison will divorce actress Gail Russell (photo at left) in Juarez, Mex., today (Tuesday) and "minutes later" will wed TV actress Sheilah Connolly, shown in photo at right with the Western star. Last week Miss Russell signed a waiver enabling Madison to obtain the divorce. Miss Connolly, ex-wife of producer Harry Danziger, met Madison last April. (AP WIREphoto)

to call her that. He didn't seem to understand that drinking was an illness. I must admit that I could not understand how someone so beautiful and successful, with a handsome husband who was also a star, could want to ruin her life with alcohol. Everyone tried to help her – even John Wayne, who wanted her for the lead in a new movie – but she couldn't do it; she just couldn't stop drinking. Then I read she drove her car into a window of a restaurant and, although no one was hurt, her driving licence was taken away. (After that, she used to ride a bike instead.)

Finally she signed the divorce papers and Guy was free. He invited me to dinner at a restaurant on Sunset Boulevard called La Rue, which was popular with the stars. We were shown to a table next to Grace Kelly and Clark Gable. They were laughing and talking excitedly. I was thrilled because I loved Clark Gable and had gone to the second première of *Gone with the Wind* with Guy. He proposed to me over dinner that night and I accepted. I was madly in love. He seemed so normal and down-to-earth for a star. He was also incredibly handsome. And he is still considered to be, it would appear. I was not surprised to see his face on the cover of a book entitled *The World's Most Beautiful Men* in 1999.

Guy and I decided to elope and we flew to Juarez, Mexico, where we were married by a justice of the peace. It was my second elopement. In Mexico the judge puts the ring on your finger when he marries you. Guy didn't like that so afterwards he took the ring off and put it on my finger again. Guy had his own way of doing things. For our honeymoon we flew on to Biscayne Bay in Florida, where Kellogg's, the sponsors of *Wild Bill Hickock,* were holding their yearly convention, which Guy had to attend. We stayed in a beautiful town house with lovely grounds by the ocean. Our honeymoon was quite short as Guy had to get back to work on a movie in Mexico.

We needed a place to live so we leased an apartment in Hollywood and planned to build a ranch-style house in the hills. Soon afterwards I found out to my delight that I was pregnant with my first child. We found a piece of land in the Outpost Estates section, a special area off Hollywood Boulevard overlooking the whole city. Guy liked its rural setting. We had plans drawn up for the house, with lots of wood panelling, Dutch doors, slate floors in the entrance, a swimming pool and of course a built-in gun case for Guy's hunting equipment. Guy designed most of the house.

In the meantime, Guy was going to make a film called *The Beast of Hollow Mountain* in Cuernavaca in Mexico so I went with him and spent a lot of time there while the house was being built. I grew to love Mexico. Then as my time grew near, I returned to Hollywood. Unfortunately, Guy was away on location in Mexico when I went into labour and he just about made it back in time for the birth of our first little blonde daughter in Los Angeles in 1955. When they took me back from the labour suite to my room in the hospital, there was Guy, fast asleep on my bed. I had to laugh. We named her Bridget Catherine since we both liked the name Bridget and my middle name was Catherine. Complete strangers, who were mostly fans of Guy, sent so many flowers to the hospital that I couldn't have them all in my room; I sent them to the other patients.

When we took Bridget home it was kind of scary at first. I had never taken care of a new baby and one day I started to walk out the door to go to the market and was almost outside when I realised that I had a baby. Someone was totally dependant on me and I couldn't leave her on her own. I missed Mama at this time. Another time when I changed her diaper, I accidentally stuck her with a pin and she screamed her head off. Guy was too afraid to change her in case he dropped her – or so he said! Little by little we adjusted to the big change in our lives and finally we settled down into a routine. When Bridget was only a month old we took her fishing down to the Colorado River. It was rather a difficult experience so I had to explain to Guy that I wouldn't be going fishing again for a while until she was older.

KEEPING TIME . . . Moving along the crowded dance floor at Romanoff's we snapped Guy Madison and his wife, Sheilah. Guy's home state is California. He fares well in both TV and screen roles. Guy and Sheilah have two little daughters, Bridget Catherine and Erin Patricia.

We were almost ready to move into our house and started shopping for furniture, but nothing ready-made was ever good enough for Guy. I was quite looking forward to my first chance to decorate and furnish a house but Guy had very definite ideas of his own. He hired a furniture-maker to craft replicas of early American chairs and tables. He was fanatical about it and we had many disagreements before I finally gave up and said he could do what he wanted everywhere else in the house but I would take over the bedrooms. I wanted something feminine somewhere in the house, so Bridget's room was pale yellow and white, our bedroom was in pale shades of blue with net curtains and the bathroom was pink. We were very happy in our new house. The last addition was a couple of rugged dogs that Guy wanted to take on his wild-boar hunting trips. I finally learnt to drive and got a station wagon so that I had room for all the baby's things. I felt so independent at last.

Several months later I found I was pregnant again. Guy was away on location a lot at this time. In his time off he hunted with the male cast in the Hickock show. They were stuntmen and were always out practising roping calves and horses. Guy considered himself to be a real cowboy! He and his friend Howard Hill used to go boar hunting in the valley off Hollywood at night because that was the best time. The valley wasn't as built-up then as it is now. Howard once killed an elephant with a single arrow in Africa. Guy was very introverted about his feelings. He didn't talk a lot but he was very concerned about proving he was a real man with the bows and arrows and guns.

In 1956, I gave birth to another girl, Erin Patricia. It

was getting hard for me to keep up with things while not being able to go to social events, so we hired a house-keeper called Eva, who had been in a concentration camp during the war. Eva was wonderful and the babies loved her. Then Guy had to go on location for a film, *On the Threshold of Space*, to be made in New Mexico, and was going to be away for some time, so I decided to go down and visit him. I knew the babies were in good hands. While I was there I met a Franciscan priest who used to visit the set. As we always had a lot of food left over from the crew he asked if he could take it to the Indian children on the nearby Mescalero mountain reservation, since they were very poor. After getting to know him I asked if I could go there with him one day and he agreed.

Tularosa was at the foot of the mountains. There I met an eighty-year-old man whose name was Robert Geronimo, the son of the famous Apache chief. I was wearing a straw sunhat and Robert liked it, so I gave it to him. The priest told me some time later he never took my hat off. I was saddened by the poverty on the reservation. The priest told me they needed a school but the banks would not give them a loan because the town of Tularosa was too small. When I returned home I started thinking about what I could do to help, so I sat down and wrote a letter. I had 500 copies made and sent out to big corporations and movie stars, enclosing stamped envelopes and ad-dressing them to the Franciscan priest, so that the money would go directly to him. The response from people like John Wayne, Glenn Ford, Eddie Albert and other actors was fantastic; large corporations sent contributions and architects offered to design the plans for the school for free. My initiative was a big success and generated enough money to get the school under way.

Shortly after Erin was born, Guy and I were asked to appear on *The Arthur Murray Show* on television in New York and the station promised to make a donation to the Apache school fund in our name. We were sent to a choreographer to learn a dance and we chose a Spanish one which I thought would be easy for Guy. We had it down pat, but when we went on stage before millions of people on national television, Guy forgot the routine and I was left to improvise. It was awful, especially since Debbie Reynolds had lent me a beautiful full-length red beaded dress which she had worn in a movie with Glenn Ford.

When they had the dedication for Tularosa in 1957, I

Louella O. Parsons in Hollywood

Home from the hunt, Guy Madison shows off his family, Erin, 10 months; Bridgit, 2, and wife Sheilah.

Guy, Bridget, Sheila and Erin on a fishing trip on the Colorado River, 1985

couldn't go because I was giving birth to our third baby, Dolly Anne. I had the children one after the other, like stepping stones. The three girls used to stop the traffic because I dressed them identically.

It was suggested at this time that Guy and I do a film together but he wouldn't hear of that at all. He didn't want me to work again after we married. I think that was to do with his Baptist upbringing and his being protective. In his book, a mother's place was at home with her children. He also left all the upbringing of the children to me but I felt I needed some kind of life outside the home. At the time, Guy was starting to get a reputation for being very difficult at work. He told a director off for using abusive language to him.

Guy was born in Pumpkin Center, Bakersfield, California. His parents were strict Baptists and they did not show their feelings or demonstrate affection even to their children. I am sure they loved them. I remember once when I was kissing the girls goodnight, Guy remarked that he didn't remembered his parents ever kissing him goodnight. We didn't have much communication with his parents except on an occasional holiday, maybe. I still remember going to visit his family for lunch shortly after we were married and, to my surprise, I discovered that Guy had an older brother, David, whom he had never mentioned before. As far as I had known, he had only two brothers, Wayne and Harold, and a sister, Rosemary. David was extremely handsome; it was hard to be better-looking than Guy but David was. He had been in the army and had become very ill. He never recovered and he talked to himself all day long. Guy didn't refer to it and neither, it seemed, did anyone else. What had happened to David was a mystery and in those days you did not question things either in the army or the family. He lived with his parents until he died.

After much persuasion, I agreed to go on a fishing trip to the Colorado River and we brought Bridget and Erin. We left Dolly with Eva because she was too young. We had gone quite far up the river when it started to get very rough. Our boat was not very big and not equipped for rough water so I became very alarmed and feared for the children. Guy wanted to continue on up the river but I could see it was really getting worse. I tried to persuade him to pull into a cove and wait but he became very impatient and insisted on going on. It was foolhardy and irresponsible but Guy was the one who made the decisions in our family and that was just the way it was. He had an expression: 'I am the ramrodder.' It was a macho thing and I am sure he did not realise how dangerous the situation might have become. He thought he could handle it. I sat on the floor of the boat with the children, who had their life jackets on, and held on to them tightly. It seemed like a lifetime until we got back. We were told that they had been on the point of sending out a rescue party and search boat for us. I was very upset by the experience and told Guy I would never go fishing again.

Things became very strained and Guy was away more and more, mostly on his hunting trips or else on film location. He invited me to Catalina Island for a break one weekend and since I didn't want anything to happen to our marriage I agreed to go with him and relax while he went wild-boar hunting with Howard Hill. The children stayed at home. While we were there he wanted me to see the boars they would be hunting. They were ensnared in a cage prior to the hunt. I went with him to the camp and suddenly the boars started charging the cage ferociously. After that I didn't want to go on any more hunts either. I felt that while I tried to fit in with his life he made no attempt to participate in mine.

I realised then that I didn't have a marriage any more; I was really alone. I told Guy I wanted a trial separation. I even thought about going back to work and was asked to test for the new *Tarzan and Jane* series. The date was set for the test and costume fitting but when Guy found out, he was so furious that I backed out.

Then Guy was offered a role in a movie in Italy. All the big directors were setting up in Via Veneto in Rome. Guy asked the children and me to join him in the Excelsior Hotel. We tried it for a week but it was unsuitable for a young family. We ended up in an a nice little villa on the Appian Way, on an estate owned by the Contessa Italico who rented out this particular villa to film stars. There were three villas next to each other and the one next to us was occupied by Walter and Verita Thompson. Walter Thompson was an Academy Award-winning editor and was working on a movie called *Come September* with Rock Hudson and Sandra Dee. Verita and I became friendly and she found two Italian girls called Titi and Nella to help me with the housekeeping and minding the children. Sidney Pollack and Bobby Darrin were friends of the Thompsons and were also in town. Bobby used to jump from their roof onto ours and sing down the chimney.

Sheila and Erin, Rome, 1960

Bobby was a fun-loving person; he would hire a horse and buggy and ride all over Rome, singing at the top of his voice until the small hours of the morning. He fell in love with Sandra Dee on that movie and they eloped. They later had one son. Poor Bobby had to have heart surgery and died of complications at the age of only thirty-five.

Guy had to go to Yugoslavia on location with Rosanna Podesta, the Italian actress, so I was left alone in Italy with the children. Guy asked me to come with him but I could not bring the children because the location was in forest country. It was difficult enough being in Italy, especially not speaking the language, let alone going to Yugoslavia to a location in the middle of the woods. When he returned, my mind was made up: I was leaving and would be filing for a legal separation. Guy stayed on in Italy to finish the movie.

The girls and I set off on our homeward journey from

Rome. En route we had a stopover in London, where we had to change planes. While we were waiting at the airport I decided to phone my ex-husband Harry at the Mayfair Hotel, which a recent newspaper article had said he owned. As luck would have it, I was able to reach him on the phone at the hotel. He said, 'Why don't you come into London?' I replied, 'Harry I can't, we're on our way back to California.' But Harry, true to form, persisted and said, 'Oh, you've got to come in and spend a couple of days in London; you can stay here at my hotel.' In the end, I relented and thought it would be nice to break the journey.

It was lovely to see Harry again after all those years. He put me and the girls up in the hotel. He'd come up and we'd sit and talk and we'd have breakfast in the room with his kids and mine, just catching up and talking about old times. His little boys were so cute. He loved my little girls. I didn't tell him about my troubles with Guy, and since Harry had never met Guy he would not have brought up the subject.

While I was in London I ran into Eddie Fisher in front of Claridge's, where he was staying with his wife Elizabeth Taylor and her children. (She had two sons by Michael Wilding and a daughter by Mike Todd.) He smiled and said, 'Hi, Irish,' which used to be his nickname for me. He said, 'Why don't you come up to our suite this evening and meet Elizabeth, and your kids can eat with hers.

I accepted. Her children were very good-looking, the boys looked like her and the girl like Mike Todd. The children were brought into another part of the suite by the nanny for their tea. Eddie led me into the drawing room and offered me a drink. Then Elizabeth made her entrance in a lovely lavender chiffon negligée with a grey Persian cat in her arms. She wasn't very well at the time and had a private nurse with her but nonetheless she looked stunning. The cat sat haughtily up on the sofa beside her and gazed at me with her pea-green eyes.

The first thing Elizabeth said to me was that I was painfully thin. I said rather defensively that I liked it that way. She didn't reply. Then she asked me if I would like to see something Eddie had given her. Naturally, I politely said I would. So she disappeared into the bedroom and sailed back in with a jewellery box in her hand. Inside was a magnificent diamond-and-emerald necklace with matching dangling emerald earrings. She tried them on. They were exquisite. She talked about her new Persian cat and said, 'People say I have cat's eyes.' Then suddenly she asked, 'Aren't you a friend of Debbie's?' It sort of threw me, but I said, 'Actually I'm a friend of both Debbie and Eddie's.' With that she made a hasty exit from the room, saying 'Excuse me' and taking her jewellery box with her. Then the nurse came out and said, 'Elizabeth won't be coming out any more this evening.' I thought Eddie was slightly embarrassed. I decided I had better leave. The kids had a great time together.

Shortly after that Elizabeth got pneumonia and almost died in London and they had to do a tracheotomy to save her. She survived and made a remarkable recovery. A month later she received an Oscar for a film called *Butterfield 8* with Eddie Fisher. Despite having a clot in her leg, she limped up for the award, only to collapse again later backstage. She was a really gutsy lady.

It was time for the girls and me to return to California. Harry was wonderful, arranging transportation to the airport for us. We said goodbye again and I thanked him for everything. 'Don't mention it,' he said, as he waved after us as we drove off. Whatever regrets I had I quickly tried to put to the back of my mind. Harry was now married with children and living in a different country and I had a divorce to sort out, three little girls to look after and a career to get back on the ground. But somehow I could never put Harry out of my mind.

17

SHARE

When I returned to Hollywood, I decided I would try an acting career again and went to see Mr Goldstein at Twentieth Century-Fox where they made a film test. Ann-Margaret was being tested on the same day. Coincidentally it turned out that we had come over to America on the same ship, the *Gripsholm*, at the same time. I was hired as one of the studio's contract players and I very much liked being on the lot. It was fun to be there and watch what was going on in the studio. They were making *The Unsinkable Molly Brown* at that time with my friend Debbie Reynolds. I used to go and visit her in her dressing room. I also met the handsome Anthony Quinn at this time. He was really friendly.

There were lots of other people under contract at that time who couldn't have been nicer. James Brolin was one of them. We both enrolled in Jack Kosslyn's Hollywood Drama School. Sometimes Clint Eastwood would come along to observe. James was very nice and kind; Barbra Streisand is very lucky to have married him and I think he's even more handsome today than he was then.

I liked being back, going to class and learning fencing, but after being at the studio for months, I realised I wasn't going anywhere and I missed being with my girls. I'd tasted the Hollywood life and now I'd had enough. I suppose the reason I wanted to go back to acting was that I felt I had lost so many opportunities because of Guy and I wanted to feel that I was worth something. I'd had three children, I was nearly thirty years old, and that in those days in Hollywood meant your career as a leading lady was nearly over. They wanted young women in their twenties.

In some ways, going back to Hollywood made me feel all the angrier with Guy because if I had got the part of Jane in *Tarzan* or taken others earlier, who knows where they might have led! If he had even met me halfway and supported me in my aspirations instead of always putting his needs first, each of us might have felt happier in the marriage. It was a really difficult phase in my life; I had to accept that I had missed the boat and a different generation of actors was emerging.

When Guy arrived back in California after his movie was finished, I tried to make our marriage work again but it was like banging my head against a brick wall; he just didn't recognise the problems. I told him I wanted a divorce and that he could spend as much time as he wanted with the children. So we filed. Afterwards, I bought a little house in Beverly Hills in a canyon, in an area very popular with the movie crowd. It was up a cul-de-sac country road in the hills, on a street called Yoakum Drive where deer, racoons and coyotes roamed free.

MADISONS LIVING APART. Actor Guy Madison, "Wild Bill Hickok" of TV fame, and his wife, the former Sheila Connolly, are on a trial separation. Madison said that there was no thought of divorce and was confident that they would be reconciled. The Madisons have been married four years and have three children. The cowboy star said that having three babies in rapid succession might have left his wife "a little tired and depressed."

For eight years, since I married Guy, I belonged to a fund-raising charity group called Share Incorporated, the Exceptional Children's Foundation. I was involved in the performances and the committee, which raised money for exceptional children. Every big star's wife was a member, and every year we put on a big show. The Boom Town Party, as it is known, is the biggest social event in Hollywood and takes place each year on 18 May. Every star in Los Angeles buys a ticket to this function. When the forty of us Share girls put on a show, we would take over the whole Civic Auditorium in Santa Monica and hold dance rehearsals every day for three months. We rehearsed a precision dance, rather like a Riverdance item, until it was perfect, under the direction of Miriam Nelson, a top choreographer and dancer in Hollywood.

In 1964, we did a trapeze act; I was one of the volunteers and we were trained by a top circus trainer for three months. Six of us had our own ladders suspended from the rafters. They swung out over the audience and we did a trapeze routine whilst swinging. There were a few mishaps and sprained wrists during rehearsals. I always got stage fright beforehand and had to run to the toilet before going up on the trapeze. Still, we were a big success and got a standing ovation. All the big male stars came and performed as well. That year I donated a beautiful rust-coloured full mink coat to be sold in the charity auction. It was supposed to be displayed by a professional model but all of a sudden Frank Sinatra walked out on stage wearing it, crowned with a tiara into the bargain! The coat went for $12,000. Another year we were booked on *The Dean Martin Show* to repeat the precision dance act on television. And guess who was appearing on that show at the same time? The Rolling Stones, on their first appearance in America. I have always had the knack of being in the right place at the right time.

At the time I was involved in Share I was also doing design work and painting. I felt I wanted to develop this, so I went to art school for a while but they weren't teaching the kind of painting I wanted to learn. They mainly taught us Rembrandt, whose dark, heavy and shadowy style was the opposite to what I wanted to create. I preferred the lighter touch of watercolours, though I ended up specialising in oils. I bought a book on how and what to paint and started teaching myself. I had never learnt to paint, even at school, so this was the first time I had never taken a paintbrush into my hands. I was really in the dark, just trying out different things.

Then, I read in an art book you should paint something you love. I looked out the window and saw my three kids playing out the back. So I thought, what could be better than to paint my kids. That was how I started. In the beginning, I couldn't wait to get up in the morning to go to work on a canvas. I became so involved with it that sometimes I found myself painting in the dark. I photographed the girls and their friends; it reached the stage that sometimes when they saw me with the camera they would run away.

In time, I built up a collection of paintings and Guy told Greg Juarez, who had a significant art gallery on Sunset Boulevard, about it. One day, Greg phoned me to say he had heard I was painting and would like to see my work. Naturally I was both flattered and delighted. I brought some canvases to his gallery and he asked if I could get enough paintings together for a one-woman show. He said I would need forty paintings to put on a show. At the time I only had about ten paintings but I said yes! He gave me a very big private showing and invited all the famous names to the opening, such as Aaron Spelling, Dick Martin and many more. John Wayne, whom I knew from Share and whose wife Pilar was a friend, agreed to write me an introduction to the catalogue. To my amazement, I sold every painting. Greg thanked me for my hard work and told me he had never seen an artist work as hard as I had done on a show. I was delighted when, later on, Sidney Sheldon, who also loved my paintings, wrote to me that I was 'an incredibly talented artist'.

I found commissions hard because I was not painting something instinctive. I found them restrictive and limiting. I felt controlled, my artistic freedom inhibited. Anyway, a lot of people preferred to buy paintings straight from my collections. Around this time I made a connection through another artist with a company in Alaska which had a string of five galleries called Stephan Fine Arts at Anchorage. They asked me to paint for them and I agreed. They had heard that I wouldn't take commissions, so they just asked me to send whatever I painted, whenever it was completed. Then I flew up and did a one-woman show. I could scarcely believe my luck. They just bought everything outright for their galleries.

One day when we were living on Yoakum Drive, my daughter Bridget came home holding a man's hand. Apparently Bridget had said to him, 'My Mommy knows you.' Then she turned to me and declared, 'Mom, you know this man,' but she had mistaken him for someone else. I said, 'I think there's been a mistake; my daughter may think I know you but I'm afraid I don't.' He smiled and agreed. He introduced himself as Robert Dowdell and I invited him in for a coffee. We had a chat and he told me was working on *Voyage to the Bottom of the Sea*. Then I realised this was how Bridget had got confused. You see, Richard Basehart, the star of the television series *Voyage to the Bottom of the Sea,* was an old friend of mine, whom I had met through Harry. We had a long conversation and soon got to know each other. It turned out that Robert (or Bob, as he preferred to be known) was a neighbour, living a few houses down from me on the same street. I couldn't help notice that he was very handsome, with his fair hair and blue eyes.

Yoakum Drive was a popular and friendly little street. My next-door neighbour was Theodore Van Runkle, who designed the clothes for *Bonnie and Clyde*. The English actress, Sarah Miles, moved into a house across from me with her small son. One day, he came to my door with some lemons for sale. He had picked them from a tree down the street and wanted a dollar for them. I went along with it and bought them. The kids used to play baseball on the street in front of our house and one day I went out with my camera. Sarah's son was just about to swing the bat and I snapped the picture and afterwards painted it. When it was finished I brought it over to her house and gave it to Sarah as a gift. She was delighted.

Bob and I continued to bump into each other on the street. One day, he arrived with a lot of firewood which he thought maybe I could use. I had a wood-burning stove, which was nice to light on cool winter nights. I was delighted at his thoughtfulness. I invited him to dinner to thank him and we became good friends. He used to invite me to functions in his friends' homes. We talked a lot and got to know each other. Eventually we became seriously involved. Bob was the total opposite of Guy: he was quieter, more sensitive and less extrovert.

Then one evening, six months later, while I was giving the children their dinner, he called around unexpectedly. When I opened the door, he immediately asked me to marry him. I was so taken aback that all I could say was 'When?' He said, 'Right away!' We were married by Judge George Dell, who presided over the Manson trial at the end of 1965. The children were not at the wedding because I thought it would confuse them but now, in retrospect, I feel perhaps they should have been there.

Sadly, I realised very soon – within the first year – that we had made a mistake. Although Bob was a wonderful person, he had mood swings. It seemed that he was searching for something that I could not give him, something he himself was uncertain about. We were not compatible and we unfortunately did not even like to do the same things. For instance, I loved to go to the beach with the kids; he didn't. I can appreciate that it was hard to go from lifelong bachelorhood to being a married man with children. We had agreed not to have any more children. The girls were growing up fast; soon it was time for them to go to public school in Westwood and later to high school in West Los Angeles. Dolly was very involved in gymnastics during high school and made it to the city finals.

Bob and I had a few friends we used to socialise with: Warren Oates, one of the stars of the movie *The Wild Bunch*, and his wife Teddy, Jock Gaynor and his wife Grace, David Hedison and Richard Basehart, whom Bridget had once thought was Bob. They were all in *Voyage to the Bottom of the Sea*.

I saw my own family from time to time. Maureen, Joan and Timmy had moved to California. Timmy went on to marry an alcoholic, a lady much older than himself, who, I suppose, was a sort of mother figure to him. In fact, because she was an alcoholic, he ended up looking after her. Timmy was not cut out for marriage, though, and it didn't last. He was too much under my father's thumb. He continued to work with horses, especially in San Diego, where they exercise on the beach. He loved going to races and loved horses. Timmy died in San Diego in 1997. He was reading a book by the ocean and closed his eyes for a moment; he never opened them again. We were all still close to him.

Not surprisingly, my father and I were never close but I felt the girls would enjoy being on a farm for a holiday. I did not feel comfortable about the idea, however, until they were old enough to keep me posted on everything. He had a place in Baltimore, Maryland, and eventually they did go to stay with him and his second wife, a woman called Sally he had married very late in life. He needed her and she needed him, I guess. She was born with one crippled arm. We didn't see that much of her. We certainly didn't consider her a stepmother. Eventually my father decided that he was too old to run a farm and he moved to California. Ironically, he was quite dependent on Maureen and Joan.

My father wasn't into horses in a big way but he would buy a horse, train it and put it in for a 'claiming' race. You have to sign a form saying that if someone wants to buy that horse and it wins, you have to sell it to them. In other words that agreement is made before the horse goes in for the race. It meant he never kept any horse for very long. This was the work that Timmy was engaged in too.

Once when my father was having a check-up in a little private hospital in San Diego, he got thirsty around ten o'clock one night. He decided to put his clothes back on and go and find a bar. Off he went and had a great time but when he got back he found that all the doors were locked. Even though he was drunk, he found his way in through Emergency and made his way to his room, where he stayed until they came to get him at 6.30 am for surgery. He said they must have found out because 'Me clothes were gone the next day.' He needed care so my sister Maureen decided that it would be OK if he and Sally came to live in San Diego. Sally and Daddy had their own house in San Diego.

He rarely came up to visit us but on one occasion when he did, I remember getting a call from the police department of Beverly Hills. They asked, 'Do you have a father by the name of Timothy Connolly?' and I feared the worst. Then they said they had him at the police station; he'd had a little too much to drink and had knocked down some big sign in Beverly Hills with his car. Yet he had such a way with him that the police even said to him on leaving, 'Have a wonderful vacation.' He always knew how to turn on the charm. That was one of my last memories of him. He died in Maureen's arms in 1981, never once having said he was sorry for what he had done to her.

Guy stayed in Italy making films and did not remarry. There was no problem about custody since he could see the girls whenever he wanted. When the girls graduated from high school, none of them wanted to follow in our footsteps into the movie world. In retrospect, I feel that Bob and I let the marriage go on too long, brushing awkward things under the carpet. We became more like brother and sister than husband and wife. And I suppose, for my part, I was very keen to preserve the marriage for the sake of the children. Bob and I did give them a happy childhood. It's very hard to admit when you have made a mistake, and so we both let it go on. Then fate intervened again.

18

WE'LL MEET AGAIN

In the summer of 1979 – the girls had grown up and left
home by now – Harry was in town and phoned me out of
the blue. I recognised that voice straight away. I said,
'Harry, where are you?' and he said, 'I'm in California and
I would like to invite you and Bob out to dinner.' Harry
also said he had heard about my painting and he asked
me to be sure to bring along some photos of my work.
When I mentioned Harry's invitation to Bob, he said he
couldn't go because he had first-aid classes but suggested
I go ahead. We went to dinner and I didn't get home until
two in the morning. We talked and talked. We had years
to catch up on. Harry himself was divorced a few years
at this stage and living in Monte Carlo. He and his brother
Eddie now owned a group of hotels around Europe and
had bought Cartier, the international jewellers, and
opened a new branch in Hong Kong. His boys, Nick and
Richard, were now at university. The next day, I took
Harry to the airport and we said goodbye again.

A few days later he phoned me from Monaco and
asked me if I could come over for a few weeks. At first I

said, 'Of course not!' Then I thought, why not? I talked it over with Bob, who reluctantly agreed. I think at the back of his mind he knew something had happened. I phoned Harry, who arranged for my ticket. I had a ball! I flew down to Nice, where Harry picked me up. I felt very happy to be back in Europe again – it felt different and exciting. Then we drove to Monaco, where Harry had a seventy-five-foot ketch in the harbour. He and his brother Eddie also had an apartment across from the Metropole Hotel.

The next day we went on the boat for a trip with a five-man crew. I had never thought of Harry as a sailor but this was a different Harry! He was relaxed and content to sit at the bow of the boat and look out to sea. I could tell he loved to sail, and I could also tell that I still loved him. The two weeks on board were absolutely wonderful: sailing from port to port, lying in the sun getting tanned, eating wonderful meals; once we picked up a chicken cooked on the spit in Italy and took it back to the boat for dinner. We played lots of different kinds of music – we both loved music. We were so happy. I couldn't believe when the two weeks were over and realised I hadn't even called home once. Harry took me to the airport and we were very quiet. We said nothing about our feelings and just whispered goodbye.

When I arrived in Los Angeles I phoned Erin to apologise for not being in touch. They had been very worried because I hadn't called. Harry phoned very soon and said he missed me already. I said I missed him too. I threw myself into my painting again, feeling very remote from everything and wanting to go back to Harry and that magical time we had had together. The next time he phoned he asked me if

I would come back to Monaco and I agreed.

I talked to Bob and told him that I felt the marriage was over. I don't think he was too surprised. It was very painful for both of us after being together for fourteen years. The girls were surprised about Bob and me breaking up but they had not been aware of the whole story. Bridget and Erin were living away from home at this point and Dolly was already married.

Harry met me at the airport in Nice and told me the boat was on its way to Gibraltar, from where they were going to make the crossing to Barbados and the Cayman Islands. We would take a plane to meet the boat and stay in Gibraltar for a little while. It was exciting being there, especially being able to live on the boat. The crossing to Spain was very rough and scary. The winds were gale force 9 – pretty rough – and I couldn't stand up. Even Eric the skipper was scared. I developed a very bad flu and cough. By the time we reached Spain, Harry decided that he and I would fly to Barbados and meet the boat there because of my illness.

Barbados was wonderful and the weather cured my flu. We went out to dinner upon arrival as one of the crew had a birthday, and we had a wonderful evening. The next day we sailed to Antigua, a great trip. The crew were a lot of fun. Unfortunately, one of the main sails was badly torn in one of the storms and we were told it would take six weeks to have it repaired. In the meantime I used to call home from the local post office, where you had to queue a long time for the phone. Because of the time difference, I was always waking someone up.

While we were in Antigua I saw a little girl about five

years old with blonde braids up in a tree and noticed that her dress had been torn right up to her underarm. I asked her what her name was and she said Jane Eyre, the name of one of my favourite books and films. I took a photograph of her up in that tree and later I painted it and sold it to the Alaska Gallery. Harry and I started running every day for exercise and we would talk about what we were going to do about our future. We agreed we would like to stay in California and live together for the time being. Not surprisingly, we were both wary of marriage.

One day a few weeks later, while we were sipping a drink on deck, an American doctor happened to come by the boat and asked Harry if he would like to sell it. Harry said sure he would and parted with the boat that very afternoon. We flew to Florida and then on to California, moving into my house on Yoakum Drive, which Bob had vacated. After a while I put it up for sale because Harry liked to go for walks and there weren't really any walks in that area. I knew I would miss the peace, quiet and rural feeling of my old house. I was sad to leave it behind.

In 1980, we bought an apartment in a gated community in Century City, where many stars such as Michael Jackson and Carol Burnett lived because of the security. We had tremendous security, so much so that when someone came to visit they had difficulty finding the person's residence. Because the complex was so spread out it took a long time to figure out the different buildings and numbers. Visitors could sometimes take up to half an hour to arrive at the door. Eventually we found the security a little too oppressive. In the meantime, Harry bought a piece of property in the Thunderbird Country

Club in Palm Springs and planned to build a large house with hand-carved doors from China, marble floors, high ceilings and a pool. The house covered 6,000 square feet. It was modern, with lots of marble and a large pool which overlooked the golf course.

One afternoon in December 1981, while I was out shopping, Harry phoned a Latino minister in downtown LA who said he could marry us that evening. When I came back home to our apartment at about 4.30 I found Harry in a state of great excitement. He said if we could make it downtown to Al's Wedding Chapel by five o'clock we could get married. We were going to have Erin come with us to the chapel but there was not enough time. The reason we had to be there by five was that Al had to marry someone in the hospital at 5.30.

I almost killed Harry! I thought it all a bit sudden; it was now 4.30 and I had about five minutes to change. I didn't have time to go out and get something new. More importantly, I didn't get a chance to invite my children along. However, I knew Harry liked to do things a certain way with minimum fuss. So we made it down to Al's, where they offered us a choice of wedding gear including a big meringue-style dress with lots of dust on it. We decided to stay dressed as we were! Al asked us what kind of ceremony we'd like and Harry said anything as long as it doesn't mention the word God. Al did very well, slipping up only once in the ceremony. Harry wouldn't answer until Al rephrased it. Then he pronounced us man and wife and when Harry smiled at me I started crying.

My daughter Erin and her husband Mark were coming

to dinner that evening. We rushed home and when they arrived I said I was sorry but dinner would be a little late because we had just got married. Erin laughed, thinking it was a joke, but Harry said it was true and told them all about it. Erin was stunned but gracefully remarked that it certainly was different. But she was happy for us, as were Bridget and Dolly.

For our honeymoon we arranged a cruise on the *QE2*, boarding at Florida in January 1982 and going round the world. It was a very luxurious trip with lots of interesting celebrities, such as George C. Scott and his then wife, the actress Trish Van de Vere, whose birthday party we were invited to on board. There was the singer Rita Moreno, columnist Art Buchwald (who was very funny) and heart surgeon Dr Christian Barnard who, when he boarded in Capetown, gave a lecture and demonstrated on-screen how he did a piggy-back heart transplant. It was really fascinating. He saved the bad heart in case the new one didn't work out.

We stopped in many interesting places; Madras in India was memorable. We went shopping in a government store where we found a life-size baby elephant carved out of a single piece of timber. It had a ceremonial ivory harness embedded into the wood, with a jewelled harness hanging from its head. It stood on a platform base of the same wood. It was a piece of breathtaking craftsmanship. Harry said he had to have it. It was part of the store but Harry started working on the salesman to convince him it would be good to have this piece of art sent to America for everyone to see. He finally succeeded. Harry was born persuasive.

The next problem was how to get it on board. It needed

QE2's ANNUAL COUNTRY FAIR

Sheila C Connolly all know as Mrs Harry Lee Danziger, pictured above, who embarked in New York for the World Cruise, has kindly donated one of her original oil paintings, which she has painted during the course of the voyage. The Painting will be raffled at Q.E.2's English Country Fair.

Some Collectors of Sheila's Oil Paintings include:

> JOHN WAYNE
> DEBBIE REYNOLDS
> BARBARA STANWYCK
> SAMMY CAHN
> CARY GRANT
> MR & MRS SIDNEY SHELDON
> HENRI MANCINI
> MR & MRS JAMES SLOAN JR
> THE KENNEDY CHILD STUDY CENTRE
> ST JOHNS HOSPITAL CALIFORNIA.

"SOME YEARS AGO, I MET A LADY WHOSE PAINTINGS I FOUND IMAGINATIVE, CREATIVE AND DELIGHTFUL. IT IS HARD FOR ME TO DEFINE IN SO MANY WORDS MY TRUE APPRECIATION OF THIS YOUNG ARTIST'S TALENT. HOWEVER, I CAN SAY THAT PILAR AND I AND MANY OF OUR FRIENDS HAVE ENJOYED OWNING "SHEILA'S". I AM SURE YOU TOO WILL BE DELIGHTED WITH "THE ENCHANTING WORLD OF CHILDREN" AS THIS ARTIST HAS CAPTURED THEM"

John Wayne

a crate and we had to get permission from the captain. That turned out to be my job because Harry reckoned the captain had a soft spot for me. Luckily I had earned some brownie points: I had painted some pictures on board and was asked by the captain to consider donating one of my works for auction for the seamen's fund. I donated two, which raised $5,000, and so he was quite happy for me to take the elephant on board, only asking how big it was. I hadn't the courage to tell him the truth, so I told him it was about knee high! He told me graciously, 'Of course, you can bring on anything you want, anything.'

In the meantime Harry was arranging for delivery of the elephant to the *QE2*. A red carpet had just been rolled out on the dock for the King and Queen of Thailand, who had just boarded. Then along came Harry with his entourage of seven little Indians followed by this big elephant in an enormous crate which could not be lifted. I couldn't believe what I saw.

I was watching the whole thing from my porthole and getting worried because we were due to sail and the captain might be upset with me when he found out. Everyone was waiting at the rails of the ship looking down in amazement. The elephant was finally heaved on board but they could only get it up to the inside of the main entrance, where it stayed during the rest of the trip. Nobody could see it because it was sitting in this huge crate. Rumours quickly circulated around the ship that the Danzigers had brought a real live elephant on board. Fortunately, when we arrived in Los Angeles we got the elephant safely through customs.

I found Hong Kong the most fascinating stop we made

on our trip. It was such a beautiful city and I loved the people. I especially enjoyed the tearooms, where you could share a table with very old Chinese people and observe their customs. I found out in Hong Kong that I was a grandmother for the second time. Bridget had given birth to a little girl while we were away and I was anxious to see them both. Frankly, I had had my share of cruising for a while. We docked in Los Angeles on 1 March 1982. Erin was waiting at the dock. Harry told me to go ahead and he would wait for them to unload the famous elephant, after which it would be transported to our house in Palm Springs, which was almost finished. The elephant was placed in the main entrance hall, where it looked spectacular.

After the trip we went back to our apartment in Century City. The house in Palm Springs was now complete but we decided we didn't want to live there because of the bad heat in the desert. We sold the house. Maybe it was because of our sailing, but we both missed living by the ocean. I told Harry I wanted to keep the elephant but unfortunately the people who were buying the house said they didn't want it unless the elephant went with it. Since we didn't have anywhere to put it and it was too big for an apartment we regretfully had to let it go with the house.

Then we decided we didn't like the confinement of living in a high-security area, so we sold the condominium and leased a quaint Cape-Cod-type house in Benedict Canyon within walking distance of Beverly Hills. Our new neighbours were Jack Lemmon, Bruce Springsteen, the Sultan of Brunei and Jay Leno of the *Tonight Show*. It was a very pretty area with lots of trees and gardens and there were lots of walks nearby for Harry.

19

Bert House

In early January 1984, we decided to take a trip to Ireland. We stayed at the Gresham Hotel in Dublin because we remembered that used to be *the* place to stay in the old days. There were newer and more chic hotels around but we decided on the Gresham, where we were treated very well. They gave us a wonderful suite the size of an apartment, with a kitchen, dining and sitting room and two bedrooms. One evening we were reading the *Irish Independent* and I happened to look at the property section. I noticed an ad for some property in Athy, County Kildare, near where I once lived. I mentioned it to Harry and he suggested we hire a car and drive down to see it. We phoned the estate agent and he told us there were forty acres for sale. So we made an appointment for a viewing the next day. It was done purely out of curiosity and we certainly had no intention of buying anything in Ireland.

On the way down, I wanted Harry to see Brownstown and I wanted to take a photo of the pump for Timmy and visit my mother's grave. It was a lovely drive through the countryside, driving past the open plains of the Curragh. I saw all the familiar places of my childhood. At Williams's corner we stopped to take pictures. I remember I was wearing a mink coat and Italian boots that day, which looked totally out of place. I showed Harry the pump where Timmy used to fetch water. It was hard to imagine how we had survived such hardships. When we wandered back to our old house it evoked such strong memories I felt as though the events had happened yesterday.

Then I found the old schoolroom where Victor died. The stone school plaque was still on the wall outside but the roof and floor had collapsed. I took a picture of the sky through the roof. Strangely there were some wee kittens with a mother cat darting around the debris on the ground and for an instant I was back there reliving that awful eviction night. I thought about my mother and how tough her life had been, and wondered again how she had ever managed to bring up so many of us. I also thought about the carefree childhood I had been able to offer my own children in comparison. I wished things had been easier for my mother.

Then we went to visit Mama's and Victor's grave, which was very overgrown with weeds. We tidied it and I left her some flowers. I had never seen my maternal grandparents' grave, although I knew they were buried around the corner in Cut Bush. Harry and I went looking for it and found a little Church of Ireland graveyard that had been desanctified and which was now for sale. There was a lovely little church with stained-glass windows in the middle of the grounds and I found the whole pastoral scene quite beautiful. There were horses grazing in the green fields beyond. It was so peaceful and quiet. The gates were chained so we climbed over the stone wall. We went from headstone to headstone until Harry found the one we were looking for right up against a wall and very overgrown. I started to pull up the weeds on their graves but Harry wouldn't let me: 'After what they did to your mother!' he said.

We continued our journey to Athy, where we met Bryan Doherty, the auctioneer. On our way out to see the property, he told us there was a Georgian period house going with the land. It never dawned on us how enormous it might be, for we didn't know its name or anything about it. I still remember our sense of expectation as we drove in the entrance and read the name Bert House on the pillars of the gates. The wheels of the car scrunched up the long gravelled avenue under the intertwining branches of the trees. Suddenly this mansion house started to loom before us. Harry and I sat in the back seat of the car not saying anything. When the car pulled up outside the entrance door we just looked at each other, wide-eyed. And then I realised that this was the mansion I had cycled past on days when I borrowed my father's bicycle and wandered off into the countryside, exploring. I used to think maybe some day if I were lucky I would get a job there as a maid.

The owners were expecting us and welcomed us inside. We were completely amazed by the size of the entrance hall, which in the old days had been a ballroom. The house dated from 1725. There was a beautiful marble fireplace at each end of the room. The walls were covered with panels of scrollwork in gold leaf, the tall ceilings

BERT HOUSE
Athy, Co. Kildare, Ireland

adorned in elaborate rococo. Long pastel brocade curtains framed the windows. To the left of the hallway was the magnificent drawing room, the French doors of which opened out onto the gardens, which sloped down towards the River Barrow. There was also a music room, which Harry loved.

To the right were all the service rooms, kitchen, breakfast room, study and two toilets, one marked Ladies, the other Gents. Down a long narrow corridor were two glass-framed doors leading into a smoking room complete with its very own private bar and upholstered leather booths. This led to a snooker room, in the centre of which was an antique snooker table complete with the original scoreboard hanging on the wall. Each room had a beautiful marble fireplace. The kitchen was down a hallway from the main dining room. I loved the big old kitchen with Georgian sloped ceilings, flagstones and a big Aga. The front main staircase swept up to the second floor, where a long corridor ran the length of the house. At the opposite end, another stairway wound its way down to the main dining room, which had five Waterford crystal chandeliers in it. It looked out on to the River Barrow, as did most of the seventeen bedrooms.

After the viewing, the owner's wife asked me if I would like a cup of tea while Harry and the auctioneer were talking to her husband. We went into the breakfast room and she brought out a tray from the kitchen with freshly brewed tea and homemade cookies. Afterwards when I came out into the hallway, Harry was visibly excited and said, 'Well, Sheila, how do you like your new home?' I was nearly in shock and asked to speak to him privately. We walked to the other end of the hallway, looking out to the garden, and I said, 'Harry, I don't want a house in Ireland – we live in America!'

'Well,' he said, 'we can sell it if you don't like it.' It was the most amazing gesture of love on Harry's part. And the best Christmas present ever! I almost burst into tears. When we left to return to Dublin, I was still suffering from shock. I could not take in the fact that I owned the house I had cycled past as a child. To me, Bert House belonged to another world. And now this was to be my world.

We flew back to the States and the contracts were sent out after us to be finalised. The children were excited and couldn't believe it! In April, we flew back to Ireland and again checked into the Gresham Hotel, hired a car and drove down to see our new home. We picked up the keys from Bryan and he brought us out for lunch. He told us the history of the house. It had formerly been the home of the Duke of Leinster. And now it was ours!

Later we drove up to Bert House and it was exciting to put our key in the front door of our new home. The views from all the windows were beautiful but my favourite was that of the River Barrow from what was to be our master bedroom. Each June the swans came down the river past our house. We drove up and down from Dublin each day to see what needed to be done. I was anxious to move in, so eventually I decided that it would be fun to get some mattresses and sleeping bags, and bunk out. As soon as we had one room fairly habitable we moved in. The weather that spring was so beautiful and unusually warm.

Every morning I woke in Bert House I wanted to pinch myself: it was like a fairy tale.

I bought a bicycle in Athy because I really wanted to ride past Bert House and pretend I was back in Brownstown. I also wanted to feel close to the countryside again, and what better way than with a bike. In the meantime, repair work to the exterior of the house, especially the roof and cornices, began. Next on the list were partial rewiring and refurbishing the bathrooms. There were also some windows and exterior doors that needed to be replaced. As with all houses, once we got started the list just seemed to grow and grow.

We started looking for the right furniture immediately; it had to be old, so we went to the auctions around the country and in the Mansion House in Dublin, picking up paintings, china and furniture. One of the estate auctions I vividly remember was held at Furness House, the home of Lady Furness, who was the fiancée of the Prince of Wales before he met Wallis Simpson. There we bought some lovely things, tables, armoires for clothes, Waterford crystal (about a hundred glasses, coincidentally in the Sheila Pattern) and a beautiful old tapestry of a garden with a couple of King Charles dogs.

I shipped over a lot of my own paintings, which we hung in the bedrooms. The house had became habitable within a few months. Most of the major repairs to the exterior were almost completed. And now we were ready to begin the painting of the exterior of the house, which was a mammoth task. They had to erect scaffolding because of the size of the house – 35,000 square feet. While this was going on, I was getting the floors sanded and varnished, and choosing colour schemes for the many rooms. People were very friendly. I dearly wanted to get a pole and put an Irish flag on it to prove that we were Irish and not English moving into the area. We were afraid they would have thought that we belonged to the diplomatic corps or something. People in Ireland (at least in the south) don't put up flags outside their homes like us Americans.

Harry had to go back to California for a few weeks on business but I decided to stay and work on the house. It seemed a good idea to invite my sisters over for a visit and Maureen and Joan were able to come. I hadn't told them how big the house was – I wanted to surprise them – and they were surprised all right! Astonished might be a better word. They thought we were sightseeing when we drove up the avenue to the big house, as they remembered it. They couldn't believe it when I told them that it was mine and that they would be staying in it for the next few weeks.

We really enjoyed ourselves. Sometimes it was painful going back to all the familiar places together. A lot of our friends had grown up and moved out of the area. However, Vi Weller, née Black, and her children were still living there. Vi and her sister Claire used to let us sneak into the picture house, you'll remember. Vi is Aunt Madge's niece.

It was during that visit that we became aware that the house might be haunted. One night Joan said she saw some strange yellow lights below her window in the garden and heard something crying like a banshee. She couldn't sleep and in the morning she had her mattress up against the door. Initially Harry and I hadn't paid much attention to the strange noises we heard when we were first there. When Joan and Maureen were leaving, Joan said she would never sleep in the house again. So there I was on my own for the next fortnight waiting for Harry to get back. Every night I heard heavy footsteps below in the hall and along the upstairs corridors. Yet I wasn't overly anxious, although I did lock the bedroom door just in case!

One night I had a terrible dream that there were rats on my bed chewing on my hands. I woke up screaming, not knowing whether it was a dream or reality. It was horrible because it reminded me of our spell in the schoolhouse when I was a child. The next morning I told Michael Gilltrap, a farmer and painter we knew, who was painting the outside of the house, about my dream. He said he reckoned I needed some cats and that afternoon brought half a dozen young cats for me to have around. I felt much happier and soon thought we needed a dog as well. I enquired around town as to where I could find a Jack Russell puppy and was told by the butcher Mr McStay that the chemist across the street had some puppies. I went over, to be told to come round to the house that afternoon when the son would show me the stock. I arrived promptly, anxious to see the dogs, and the son took me to a medieval building hidden from the street at the back of their house which turned out to be a primitive gaol. The old building where the puppies were living had iron bars on the windows and there were lots of little cubicle cells. In one of the cold stone cells was a mother dog with a litter of five or six Jack Russell puppies. I was so taken with them that I took two for £30.

I immediately brought them to the vet for shots and he recommended I give them a nice warm bath. They looked so cute and followed me everywhere like shadows. One I named Tuppence and the other Penny. I bought them two lambskins for bedding and let them sleep by the Aga. When Harry finally arrived back early one evening and I went outside to meet him, the two little Jack Russells came charging out with me, and he smiled because they were so cute.

The dogs and cats were thriving: Penny and Tuppence went hunting daily in the garden, chasing hares and pheasants. Harry wanted to shoot some pheasants in the grounds but I said that no one was allowed to hunt on our property; besides, the animals were doing a good enough job! Sometimes the dogs caught a hare in the garden. More often than not they chased rats along with the cats and were constantly depositing their kills as presents at our front door.

One day I was taking Penny and Tuppence for a walk on our road when they disappeared through the fence. Soon they came running back all covered with cow shit, chased by a herd of charging cows. I was about to climb into the next field but there were horses also running towards us on that side. They were curious to know what all the fracas was about, I guess. I was forced to picked up the smelly dogs and run home as fast as I could, with one under each arm. I threw the dogs into a tub of water in the laundry room and gave them a bath, though the smell of them nearly knocked me over.

Harry is the gentlest person with animals. When he

opens a can of dog food he doesn't just dump it on a dish; he arranges it as if he were preparing a gourmet meal. One evening he was reading in bed. It was a very cold night and I had made us mugs of cocoa with a little brandy in it. The dogs were lying on the floor of our bedroom and I placed my mug on a low table which I thought was beyond the reach of the dogs and went to get ready for bed. When I came back the dogs were on the bed and my cocoa was finished. The dogs had drunk it and become very feisty. They started fighting, and, Harry's thumb accidentally getting in the way, he was bitten. There was blood all over the duvet. I jumped onto the bed to try and separate them. Harry got Penny and threw her into the hallway. I threw the duvet over Tuppence and pushed her into the bathroom. 'Those dogs will never have a drop in them again,' I said. When I asked how Harry's thumb was he just shrugged and said they didn't mean any harm: 'They were just drunk, the little blackguards!'

Michael Gilltrap had some bullocks which he put in one of our fields to top the grass. We had a beautiful rose garden in the roundabout in front of the house and one night they broke out and ate all the tops off the roses. I closed the gate and corralled them there so they wouldn't wander onto the main road; then I went out looking for Michael. I finally found him at Reggie's pub drinking a pint of Guinness. When I told him what had happened he said with a big grin, 'Well, you might say they're smelling like roses!'

The house was really looking well and what we needed then was some help. We soon found out we didn't have to go looking for it because the first person to ring our door was a man called Jimmy, who introduced himself early one morning, so early that I wasn't even properly dressed. When Harry asked him to come in Jimmy looked down at the wooden floor and said, 'Oh what a pleasure it would be to polish these floors!' Harry ran up the stairs to get me, calling out excitedly, 'Sheila, you've got to come down; there's a real live leprechaun at the door!' I threw on my robe and went downstairs, and when Jimmy told me that he used to ride his bike past Bert House every day and hope some day he might get a job as houseman there, I looked at Harry with tears in my eyes and we both nodded. His story was so like my own. 'When would you like to start, Jimmy?' asked Harry, and it was agreed that he would start the next day. Then I asked him if he would like to cook and he said he would love to. We were absolutely delighted; later we were to discover the accuracy of this remark; what he meant was that he would love to *know* how to cook!

Jimmy arrived early the next morning and I watched from my window as he rode his bicycle up the avenue. He was wearing a suit and tie and a hat, and carried an umbrella on the handlebars. The bullocks became quite lively and ran towards the fence near him, so Jimmy shook his umbrella at them and shouted abuse. It was a very funny scene and I remember thinking to myself how much I loved being here! One day I sent Jimmy into town for a lamb roast at McStay's butchers. He borrowed my bike because his own had a flat tyre. McStay asked him what he wanted with a lamb roast. Jimmy told him it was for Bert House and the butcher was completely amazed to discover that he was now our butler. Jimmy had a great time, especially when some men who had overheard news of his proud new position asked how had he got the job and could he get them one too. He refused them all!

Jimmy told Harry that his sister Mary had been cook for the More O'Ferralls since she was sixteen years old. She worked for them for forty-five years. Jimmy shared a house with her and when the More O'Ferralls had a sit-down dinner for a lot of people, Dinkin the butler used to ask Jimmy to help out. When Jimmy got home from the butcher's we asked him again if he could cook. He was vague in his reply. One day I asked him what he liked to cook, because he hadn't cooked anything except porridge since his arrival and it was then that he said he would love to cook but didn't know how! He had taken us so literally we couldn't be angry.

I realised, then, we would have to find someone to cook. Fortunately for us around that time a young girl called Terry came to the door saying that her father was a porter at the bank and she would like a job. We needed somebody for housekeeping so we employed her. Then it turned out that Terry's friend, Catherine, who was taking Cordon Bleu cookery lessons, was also looking for a job. She came to work for us as a cook during the summer. It was a great arrangement – they got along very well and were always laughing and giggling together. It was lovely to be able to go to Dublin for the day and arrive home to find a roast stuffed chicken with potatoes in the oven, a porter cake and freshly made soda bread.

And they would always leave a note to say that the 'little savages' were fed. This was how they referred to our dogs because of their hunting habits.

Unfortunately, Catherine could stay with us only for a few months because she got accepted for veterinary school. We lost a fantastic cook and friend, and I began to wonder how we would cope without her. Then the Dohertys (Bryan Doherty was the real-estate agent who had sold us the hourse) told me they had a relative called Joan who was just finishing at the Cordon Bleu school. Joan came to work with us. She very nearly didn't take the job because Catherine and Terry scared her by telling her she would have to go down to the cellar every day to do chores. They also told her the cellar was haunted. Fortunately Joan had a good sense of humour and soon realised they were only teasing. We got on well with Joan, she was a great cook and it worked out fine. She was also very pretty.

Jimmy was a very funny person, not the sort to stand on ceremony. I remember an incident at a very formal luncheon being given by the More O'Ferralls. An important titled dignitary was present and had run out of cigarettes. Jimmy, the ever-helpful butler, pulled a packet out of his own pocket and said, 'Here, have a fag,' slapping him on the back. He wasn't a very formal butler but at the same time he was always very courteous.

We decided we needed an established butler at Bert house to help train in Jimmy. A man who had worked for Lord Iveagh applied for the job. Harry thought he would be just right, even though he took himself very seriously. One day when Catherine and Terry were doing chores upstairs, he came to me and said, 'Where I was employed the scullery maids stayed in the scullery.' Somehow that remark stung. That afternoon I drove him to the bus stop along with his suitcase. Jimmy told me later that he had been ordered to serve him tea in bed every morning but hadn't wanted to tell me. That day Jimmy was unusually happy and whistling around the house. He looked up to us: 'I used to think of you as my employers but now I think of you as my parents.' It was quite touching. We were very fond of him and it was a compliment to us that he used to put his Irish dancing trophies all over our antique fireplaces in the hallway.

After we had finished all our renovating and decorating, we let it be known that everyone in the village was welcome to come up and visit. The nuns from the local convent were the first to arrive. I don't think they were very kind to Jimmy in his schooldays, for when he saw them he turned to me and asked if he had to serve them tea. I told him he didn't – so he didn't. When we came to live in Athy, I often used to draw up in my car outside the convent in Naas where I stayed but I could never bring myself to go in. I intended to go in but I couldn't. It was as if I were paralysed in my car and couldn't move.

One day Catherine was vacuuming upstairs and came running down to say that she had suddenly felt the presence of something and the hair on the back of her neck had stood up. After that incident none of the staff would go up to a room alone or even contemplate going down the cellar. I have to say I didn't blame them. The cellar was definitely a very creepy place, especially at night, so I never went down there. It was enormous, all floored and walled in stone with little rooms with great big heavy wooden doors which reminded me of some kind of primitive prison cells. There was a wine cellar with stone shelves and a door with a large keyhole that made a scary creaky noise when the key was turned. Then there was a stairway that went nowhere – it ended at the ceiling. From the cellar there was door out into a courtyard that was obviously used in the old days to bring in the carriages.

We could never explain these visitations and, surprisingly, though of course we continued to lock my bedroom door, they never really 'freaked me out'. Night after night, we used to hear the sound of someone coming up the stairs. Then we heard from our gardener a story about Bert House in the old days. One of the gardeners had looked through the window of the main hall and seen an apparition of a nun sitting by a fire. Then she had faded away.

Strange things continued to happen at Bert House: two small shades flew off some wall sconces for no reason and once, while we were having lunch in the small dining room, there was a loud crash in the music room – a watercolour of a Protestant church in Northern Ireland crashed to the floor, breaking the glass, but the hook was still on the back of the frame and the wall hanger was intact.

Then Alistair Hamil, who came to take over the stables, told us about an experience he had had, while staying at the house alone. One night at about two am he was wakened by the sound of a baby crying in the hall. He got up and listened at the door and heard some women singing in Irish. He opened the door and called out, thinking Jimmy had come home. Suddenly all sounds stopped. It was soon after that, while Alistair was staying at Bert House in the room beside Jimmy's, that we found out that he wasn't actually living in; he was too scared. Instead he rode my bicycle to work at six o'clock every morning before we got up so we never missed him. We didn't mind because we just wanted him to stay, we were so fond of him.

One evening we arrived home, having been out to a dinner party. There was something white running back and forth in front of the entrance making strange sounds. We called out, 'Who's there?' but the movement just continued. We were quite afraid and started to get back into the car when suddenly Alistair came out from under a white sheet. He really frightened us but we had to laugh.

Harry wanted to get the stables up and running and keep a few horses. We had met Homer Scott, who was in the racing business and was the owner of Lisheen Stud in Castledermot near Athy. We became friends with him and his wife Fionnuala, who was quite beautiful. Through Homer we found Alistair Hamil, who used to work with the Queen's horses in England; he took over the stables and bought some racehorses for us. He also ran our stud farm, which had eighty-six boxes. We had two cottages down by the stables so it was ideal for a stud-farm manager because he could live in one and convert the other into an office.

Initially the stables were in a poor state of repair. Little by little, we turned these grounds into a top-ranking stud farm, which housed facilities that were undoubtedly the best in Ireland. We spent almost two years preparing the ground. We split the land up to facilitate the management of mares and foals and built an enclosed indoor arena and covering barn where yearlings could be broken in and stallions could cover mares. We were especially proud of the secluded stallion yard, which had its own private entrance, thus doing away with the problem of stallions passing through the mares' stable area. The stallions' box even had infra-red lamps!

We housed some famous mounts like the top-class miler Mr Fluorocarbon, trained by the renowned Henry Cecil at Newmarket and winner of the 1988 Queen Anne Stakes at Royal Ascot. The filly Impressive Lady was also in our stables. She was a first-time-out winner at the Crush, trained by Liam Browne of the Curragh and now owned by trainer Dermot Weld. The paddocks had wind-breakers which offered added shelter to young stock. The stable area now had seventy-one boxes, most of which were filled. The mares had a special foaling treatment room, with adjacent foaling boxes also fitted with infra-red lamps to provide warmth to mare and foal. We saw lots of births during our time there, which I always found very exciting. It was wonderful to see that little foal stand up right away and go to feed off its mother.

Most impressive of all was our Danziger Aqua Track, designed by Harry and Alistair. It was the first of its kind in Ireland and was essentially an underwater treadmill. This way injured horses could exercise painlessly, under the therapeutic effect of jacuzzi jets, and be restored to top condition. We bought a couple of horses to train and race. One of them was a big strong stallion, and because I loved the song 'Come Back, Paddy Reilly' we decided to register him as Ballyjamesduff. The first race this horse ran he won by eight lengths. Everyone in the stands was singing 'Come back Paddy Reilly to Ballyjamesduff'. It was a really wonderful day.

Since we never turned anyone down we had quite a few people working for us, especially at the stables because the stud farm was so large. We gave a lot of work to the local community, especially to boys who had left school early. Somehow working with animals seemed to give them confidence and self-belief. One boy in particular became a really good rider and went on to get other jobs. These boys knew nothing about horses when they came to Bert House. We were very friendly with our stable boys; it was not like in America, where one boy rides, another boy feeds.

An elderly retired man who was still very fit and anxious to work approached us one day. When Alistair asked him what he could do the man replied, 'Anything; anyting.' And so he became our gardener, and pretty soon he looked ten years younger. He also became a father figure for the boys who worked there and who were troubled. Jimmy told me our house had a nickname. 'Oh what's that?' I said. 'They call it the orphanage,' he said.

Harry had never been on a horse before so Terry, who worked with us, told us about a riding school nearby. I went there and found out they were going on a ride the next day and we could go with them. I explained that Harry had no previous experience so they said they would give him a quiet, easy horse. When we arrived, I was slightly alarmed when the manageress brought out a stallion for Harry. I was expecting an old horse; imagine putting a new rider up on a stallion. Poor Harry! However she assured me the horse was harmless. We started out across the fields on a cross-country trek. When we reached the first stream, Harry's horse took it into his head to go down on his knees and splash water on his belly. Poor Harry looked like he was riding a bucking bronco at this stage, but worse was to come as we continued through a forest with lots of fallen trees, where the horses had to find their way over large branches and other obstacles. It certainly wasn't what you would expect on your first time out. As we trekked rode home on the road, poor Harry was pretty tired and saddle-sore. He turned and asked me whether we had much further to go. It was a pretty tough ride.

20

—

ATHY AND AFTER

Alistair wanted to start a little entertainment club on the side in Athy. He found a place to lease and, as he was friendly with the singer Bob Strong and his wife, he was able to persuade Bob to sing. He in turn brought his fourteen-year-old son Andrew along to perform as well. Andrew was the star of the show and brought the house down. It was no surprise that he later became a big star in the film *The Commitments*.

Mrs Clancy's pub parlour was the place to go on Thursdays in Athy. Musicians came from all over to perform on violin, flute and accordion, as well as to recite poetry. Harry played the violin so he was welcomed to the group. They were wonderful evenings because there were people with remarkable talent: people reciting poetry, a little girl playing the flute who, given the chance to be trained in Dublin would really have made it, and a fiddler who reluctantly gave his fiddle to Harry for him to play. And they said that when Harry played it, Mrs Clancy (who must have been in her eighties) fell madly in love with him. They used to tease Harry and call him her boyfriend.

They were all drinking like mad as well. You would see twelve pints lined up on the table.

There was this one guy, a farmer, who was brilliant at reciting poetry, especially that of Yeats. Harry told him if he ever thought of going to Las Vegas, he could fix it for him. And he said to me, 'Boy, I'm an old man in my eighties; I'm not going any place. What would I want to go to Las Vegas for!' He would have been a smash, with his wonderful brogue and his talent for performance.

Encouraged by Mrs Clancy's musical evenings, I decided I wanted to learn how to play the flute and sound like James Galway! I bought a flute and took lessons from a young flautist called Justin Kelly from the town. I didn't realise how difficult it was to play and to read music, and although Harry used to help me at the piano, playing along with me, I would become impatient and want to play tunes instead of studying the scales. Harry said I had no sense of discipline in my approach to learning. I suppose this was a throwback to my schooldays. I had never learnt how to study because of our random schooling. I found I couldn't learn unless I did it my way and on my own, and the thought of being in a class made me panic. I had always been terrified of school in Ireland because I couldn't understand my lessons, and the trauma of being punished in front of the class will remain with me to my dying day. I was not very good at the flute and gave it up when I started having a respiratory problem.

My second daughter, Erin, her husband, Mark, and their two-year-old son, Justin, came for a visit in the late summer of 1986 on their way back from Sweden. Mark was a soil engineer who measured earthquakes. The weather was frightful during their visit but Erin said somehow it was really beautiful and colourful. They were fascinated by the changeability of Irish weather. They couldn't get over the frequency with which sunshine became rain. Mark was particularly taken by the amount of cloud, fascinated by the way the clouds were always scudding across the sky. Sometimes we had severe storms with thunder and lightning without warning. It was very different for them. Even I had forgotten how varied the weather could be after all my years in the States. Not surprisingly the weather is always a topic of conversation with people in Ireland.

Justin was an adventurous and independent child. On the very first morning he found his way down to the kitchen by himself. He knew exactly where to go. Little boys love food! He used to go up to the racehorses on his own and he also loved cows. The dogs and cats were also mad about him and used to follow him everywhere he went. He looked like the Pied Piper at times. Justin is now a mature and sensitive teenager, and he works after school for a criminal attorney in Beverly Hills. I used the opportunity of her visit to take Erin to visit the grandparents' graves. She has recently completed her computer studies and is working in the music industry Unfortunately, Mark died tragically of breast cancer in 1993.

Bridget also came over to visit in the autumn of that year with her two children, Simone and Spencer. The children went riding and fishing on the river running through our grounds and they had a wonderful time. Harry didn't go fishing, which was a pity because we had

Sheila with Simone and Spencer at Bert House, 1986

our own fishing deck right at the back of the house. The problem was that the minute you put your line in the water, it got caught in the river's many reeds. Harry just didn't have that kind of patience. A lot of people used to fish further down the banks on our property.

One night during Bridget's visit, because it was incredibly bright even though it was almost ten o'clock, she decided to go up and close the inside shutters so that the children would not think it was morning. When she went into the room the shutters were open but when she turned round from checking that Simone and Spencer were all right, the shutters had closed. She also heard knocking on the third floor during the night. Yet she wasn't afraid; somehow she sensed that it was a friendly ghost.

Despite this encounter with our ghostly presence, Bridget loved the country so much that she actually started toying with the idea of leaving California and living in Ireland. I told her I didn't think it was such a great idea because her career and life were in California. After she came back from a Christy Moore concert in Athy, I had even more trouble dissuading her from uprooting. When they were leaving, they were all in tears. Simone was devastated at the thought of leaving the horses behind.

Dolly and her family were also due to come over but they changed their minds because of the Lockerbie air disaster of December 1988. They were frightened because of the worldwide terrorism of the time and the troubles in Northern Ireland. Dolly is married to Robert Stondell; they have three children, Jessie, Casey and Chelsea, who are now teenagers. They live in Northern California. Over ten years ago Dolly decided to go back to college to study medicine. She had had her children by that stage and, luckily for her, Robert, her husband, worked from home. She is now a doctor at a hospital in Sacramento.

We made a lot of friends in Ireland; they were an interesting, eclectic bunch. Our closest friends were Homer and Fionnuala Scott of Lisheen and the real-estate agent Bryan Doherty, and his wife Daphne, whom we loved. They were all extremely good company.

After a while, we got used to our new way of life. Some mornings, I would get up and ride out across the fields in the early-morning dew. The dogs would run behind me chasing rabbits and hares in my wake. The odd time, I would join one of the jockeys on their ride-outs, but more often than not I preferred the freedom of riding alone. Then I would come back totally invigorated to one of Catherine's special Irish breakfasts or one of Harry's frothy omelettes and together we would listen to *The Gay Byrne Show*. Sometimes Alistair would join us and we would have a breakfast meeting to discuss the horses. Then I would draw up my list of shopping and discuss menus with Catherine or Joan and head down to Athy.

In those days in Ireland, shopping expeditions into town were a big thing. It was wonderful to be able to get such fresh ingredients. I would go to the butcher's shop, the fruit and vegetable shop and, of course, I stopped in a whole string of other shops and chatted to everyone in the street as I went along; it was very much a social thing. Other mornings I might go for coffee with Fionnuala. In the afternoons, I used to ride my bike along country lanes and pick wild flowers. I also used to love rambling across the fields with Tuppence and Penny. In the early years, I was out at auctions quite a bit, travelling all over the country. I used to love listening to the radio in Ireland on my trips around the country and I particularly loved Marion Finucane. I thought her programme brought me closer to understanding the Irish. It seemed to capture the spirit of contemporary Ireland. In the autumn, we used to go blackberry-picking and Harry would make the most delicious blackberry pies.

There is an interesting photographer, John Minihan, from Athy; he now lives in London. He still comes back to Athy to do photo studies of people he knew when he was growing up there. A typical subject was old Julie Mahon, who was thin and very wiry. She rode her bicycle everywhere and always wore the same hat. She used to visit her mother's grave every day, and bring her lunch with her. Then she would sit down by the tombstone and greet her mother with, 'Well, how's it going?'

One day I had a very unpleasant experience. Just after I had finished doing my shopping in the supermarket in Athy, I opened my back door to put my groceries on the back seat of our car. Unfortunately, because of our British number plates, we were sitting ducks at that time in Ireland. Suddenly some men surrounded me. I thought they were going into the store but they stayed around the car. I tried to move to get into the car but they stood in my way and said they'd like to ask me a few questions first. They weren't young but quite mature, in suits and ties. 'What kind of questions?' I asked, slightly alarmed by their tone. I thought, 'If you want to ask me any questions you can follow me home in my car and you can speak to my husband.' They asked me where I lived and I said, 'I live here.'

I was trying to figure out how I could get away from them so I just dashed between them and ran back into the supermarket. I told the manager that they wouldn't let me get into my car and asked him if I could phone my husband. I thought the store manager would call the police but he was very casual about it all and didn't bother to do anything. Within minutes of my phoning Harry, both he and Alistair came charging into the car park in the jeep. The men were still sitting on the bonnet of my car. They wanted to know where we had got the car but when they heard Harry's accent and ascertained we were not British, they changed their attitude. Not that they apologised or anything. They just said they were from the customs but we could hardly believe that customs men would behave like that. Genuine customs men would surely have shown some me identification to calm my fears.

It was now almost six years since we had first moved to Bert House. We felt very settled and had collected lots of nice things. A young art-gallery owner on Molesworth Street called Angela Nugent helped us a lot because she had a good eye and was a great collector herself. She was very interested in horses and we would regularly meet at the Curragh. She was lots of fun.

I had always wanted an old-fashioned pony and trap, like the ones people used to travel around in during the thirties and forties. Alistair found one in very good condition for me at a nearby farm. Then we acquired a beautiful grey pony with a long white tail and mane. Its name was Beauty, even though it was a he. The first day we hitched him up to the trap and took him out on the road he went crazy, bucking and kicking. I got out while Alistair walked the pony home. Beauty was so lively; he would try to fight with the thoroughbreds in the fields. In the end, I just gave up. Angela Nugent loved the pony and wanted the trap so she bought them from us. So that was the end of my pony-and-trap episode. I think Beauty must have eventually quietened down, away from the thoroughbreds.

Harry and I went on a short vacation to France. Harry had seen some bicycles with motors in a magazine that he thought would be ideal for the stable boys to ride to work on. We bought two and put them in the back of the car. When we arrived at Irish customs an official looked in the car and remarked that we must be going to tour Ireland by bicycle. Harry said we were, and the official just waved us on. When you consider our ages and how difficult such a journey would have been for us, we thought it was quite a compliment to us both, aside from the advantage of not having to pay duty!

The next day, Harry began to demonstrate to the boys how to use the bicycle. However, when Harry got on the bicycle and turned on the motor he took off and disappeared through the bushes. They were all waiting for him to come back, thinking that this was part of the demonstration, but poor Harry was in fact lying on the ground on the other side of the bushes, having been thrown off the bike. 'Forget the bicycles,' he said. 'No one is ever going to ride them.' And no one ever did.

We often used to head off in the car as part of our plan of discovering Ireland. We went to Waterford and bought a lot of Waterford glass. In Kilkenny we fell in love with the castle and the Kilkenny Design Shop, where we bought lots of gifts of linen, sweaters and wool capes. I built up a collection of Jimmy Hourihan capes which I loved. We often used to visit Kinsale in County Cork, and enjoyed the seafood restaurants, and we loved Inch in Kerry, where they made the film *Ryan's Daughter*. It had the most stunning stretch of golden sand I have ever seen. We loved going for long walks there.

During this time I started having respiratory problems. My condition became progressively worse – I thought I was on the way out – and it meant my having to make emergency trips from Athy to St James's Hospital in Dublin, a journey that was no joke. Then we discovered that the house had weeping walls because we were near a river and this dampness was activating my chest complaint. Finally my doctor, Luke Clancy, suggested that I should consider going back to a warmer, drier climate. When Harry and I discussed it, we realised that if I was to get well, we had to leave Bert House. There really was no option. Reluctantly we put Bert House up for sale and a buyer was found.

It broke our hearts when the day came to depart – we left everything in the house, even my paintings. It was an awful wrench. Angela Nugent was almost as devastated because she had helped me source many unusual antiques for the house and we had had so much fun together at the auctions. We realised that if we started making exceptions we would end up taking everything. So we sold the house and contents, church, cemetery and acreage to the lucky buyer! We walked through the house many times, wanting to imprint memories of all the rooms on our minds. We left our two family crests, Connolly and Danziger, on the back of the two glass doors of the atrium, so there would always be something of us there. Penny and Tuppence, our beloved Jack Russells, stayed on in Athy in a good home, where we know they are very happy, but we still miss them. We had to leave the dogs behind because they were used to roaming freely around all that land and it would not have been fair to them suddenly to find themselves cooped up in an apartment. We especially miss Jimmy, our friends and of course the house itself. I will never forget Bert House.

Korean War Memorial Award 1990

If I hadn't got sick we would still be in Ireland today. As it was, I left left Athy for America in 1990, heading back to California with Harry. We now divide our time between Los Angeles, where my children and grand-children live, and Mexico, where we have a house on the beach. We are incredibly happy and content together. Harry has plans for our final resting place – Arlington National Cemetery, where American war heroes rest. But a little piece of my heart will always remain in Ireland.

Reunion in 1993 of girls who were models in New York in the 1950s: from left (back): Betty Murray, Lorraine Knopf, Sheila; (front): Helen Ryan, Daphné Doré, Tippi Hedron, of The Birds *movie*